The Quotable
Aquarius

The Quotable Aquarius

Aquarius Traits
Described by Fellow Aquarians

Usual birthdates
January 20 through February 18

Mary Valby

Quotable Zodiac Publishing, LLC
Gig Harbor, Washington

The Quotable Aquarius
Aquarius Traits Described by Fellow Aquarians

Quotable Zodiac Publishing, LLC
Post Office Box 2011
Gig Harbor, WA 98335 USA
Orders@QuotableZodiac.com, www.QuotableZodiac.com

Although the author and publisher have made every effort to ensure the accuracy and completeness of information contained in this book, we assume no responsibility for errors, inaccuracies, omissions, or any inconsistency herein. Any slights of people or organizations are unintentional.

ISBN 978-1-936998-11-1

Design & layout: BookDesign.ca
Printed in U.S.A.
Distributed by SCB Distributors

With appreciation for my favorite Aquarians
Olin and Casey

He sees his species as kindred.
Thomas Paine, born 2/9/1737

I want people to have the grandest vision for their lives.
Oprah Winfrey, born 1/29/1954

Contents

Author's Notes about Birth Data

Data accuracy. Many famous people have different birth years published in different places. The author has checked multiple sources for accuracy and asks that reliable data corrections be submitted to info@quotablezodiac.com.

Old Style / New Style dating. All countries in the Western world shifted from the Julian (Old Style or O.S.) to the Gregorian (New Style or N.S.) calendar, jumping ahead up to 12 days to catch up with the actual movements of the Sun. The timing of the change varied significantly by country, with France adjusting in 1582, England in 1752, and Russia in 1918. All birthdates in *The Quotable Aquarius* use New Style dating to accurately reflect the astrological position of the Sun.

"On the cusp." The usual dates for an Aquarius Sun are January 20 through February 18. But the Sun moves from Capricorn to Aquarius and from Aquarius to Pisces at a specific moment each year, with the dates varying by a day or two from year to year. In the effort to include only true Aquarians in this book, the author evaluated place of birth and time of birth where available. If you were born on the cusp and are unsure about your own Sun sign, email your date, time and place of birth to help@quotablezodiac.com for a free identification.

Introduction

Y ou know you're an Aquarian. You identify with the standard adjectives used to describe Aquarius—inventive, humanitarian, eccentric, free. But you'd like more dimension to what being an Aquarian means.

The Quotable Aquarius lets your fellow Aquarians tell your story. Famous Aquarians describe your natural Talents for individuality and vision in one chapter, addressing Challenges like temper and aloofness in another. The section on Double-Edged Traits highlights Aquarian characteristics like unpredictability and independence that become strengths or weaknesses depending on expression. Chapters about Work, Creativity, Sports, and Relationships let you focus on Aquarius tendencies within a specific arena. The core Aquarian traits of intellect, objectivity and breaking barriers come through in all areas. *The Quotable Aquarius* lets you select Aquarian leaders, artists and athletes to identify with as you develop your own Aquarius potential.

The astrological placement of Sun in Aquarius at your moment of birth indicates your core energy, the life force driving the rest of your personality. From classic literature to contemporary celebrities, statements from other Aquarians underscore your natural tendencies. It goes beyond coincidence that popular, visionary Aquarius contributes more U.S. Presidents than any other zodiac sign. The Water-Bearer's involvement in social issues leads to an extensive list of famous Aquarian causes. Aquarian innovation and genius correlate with the zodiac's highest concentration of superstar athletes.

Astrology is most useful as a tool for self-knowledge, validating specific tendencies that you already perceive in yourself. Astrology describes the hand of cards that you were born with, but you put the cards into play. *The Quotable Aquarius* helps you better understand yourself so that you manage your Aquarian tendencies more effectively to achieve your goals.

Aquarius Birthday Calendar

January 20		January 21	
1956	Bill Maher	1743	John Fitch
1965	Sophie Rhys-Jones	1813	John Fremont
		1824	Stonewall Jackson
		1884	Roger Baldwin
		1895	Cristobal Balenciaga
		1905	Christian Dior
		1922	Paul Scofield
		1925	Benny Hill
		1940	Jack Nicklaus
		1941	Placido Domingo
		1941	Richie Havens
		1946	Gretel Ehrlich
		1947	Jill Eikenberry
		1951	Gregory Itzin
		1953	Paul Allen
		1956	Geena Davis

January 22		January 23	
1561	Francis Bacon	1598	François Mansart
1588	John Winthrop	1783	Stendhal
1690	Nicolas Lancret	1832	Edouard Manet
1788	Lord Byron	1862	David Hilbert

1875	D.W. Griffith	1898	Sergei Eisenstein
1909	Ann Sothern	1899	Humphrey Bogart
1909	U Thant	1928	Jeanne Moreau
1910	Harold Geneen	1938	Hugh Prather
1913	Carl F.H. Henry	1957	Princess Caroline (Monaco)
1932	Piper Laurie	1964	Mariska Hargitay
1940	John Hurt	1974	Tiffani Thiessen
1959	Linda Blair		
1965	Diane Lane		
1975	Balthazar Getty		
1985	Orianthi		

January 24		January 25	
1670	William Congreve	1759	Robert Burns
1712	Frederick the Great	1874	W. Somerset Maugham
1732	Pierre Beaumarchais	1882	Virginia Woolf
1860	Bernard Kroger	1933	Corazon Aquino
1862	Edith Wharton	1981	Alicia Keys
1883	Estelle Winwood		
1888	Vicki Baum		
1917	Ernest Borgnine		
1918	Oral Roberts		
1941	Neil Diamond		
1949	John Belushi		
1968	Mary Lou Retton		
1972	Allison DuBois		
1974	Ed Helms		
1986	Mischa Barton		

January 26		January 27	
1826	Julia Grant	1741	Hester Lynch Piozzi
1880	Douglas MacArthur	1756	Wolfgang Amadeus Mozart
1905	Maria von Trapp	1832	Lewis Carroll

1918	Nicolae Ceausescu	1850	Sam Gompers
1921	Akio Morita	1885	Jerome Kern
1925	Paul Newman	1893	Soong Ching-ling
1928	Roger Vadim	1921	Donna Reed
1944	Angela Davis	1948	Mikhail Baryshnikov
1946	Gene Siskel	1959	Keith Olbermann
1957	Eddie Van Halen	1963	Arpad Busson
1958	Anita Baker	1964	Bridget Fonda
1958	Ellen DeGeneres		
1961	Wayne Gretzky		
1970	Kirk Franklin		

January 28 / January 29

1225	Thomas Aquinas	1843	William McKinley
1814	Eugene Viollet-le-Duc	1860	Anton Chekhov
1873	Colette	1880	W.C. Fields
1912	Jackson Pollock	1882	Berton Braley
1936	Alan Alda	1939	Germaine Greer
1955	Nicolas Sarkozy	1943	Katherine Ross
1968	Sarah McLachlan	1945	Tom Selleck
1977	Joey Fatone	1954	Oprah Winfrey
1980	Nick Carter	1968	Edward Burns
1981	Elijah Wood	1970	Heather Graham
1982	Camila Alves	1982	Adam Lambert
		1985	Athina Onassis

January 30 / January 31

1775	Walter Savage Landor	1797	Franz Schubert
1882	Franklin Roosevelt	1875	Zane Grey
1920	Delbert Mann	1881	Irving Langmuir
1922	Dick Martin	1892	Ugo Betti
1925	Dorothy Malone	1893	Freya Stark
1928	Ruth Brown	1902	Tallulah Bankhead

1931	Gene Hackman	1915	Thomas Merton
1937	Vanessa Redgrave	1919	Jackie Robinson
1941	Dick Cheney	1921	Mario Lanza
1951	Phil Collins	1923	Carol Channing
1951	Charles Dutton	1923	Norman Mailer
1958	Brett Butler	1937	Philip Glass
1962	Abdullah II (Jordan)	1940	Stuart Margolin
1974	Christian Bale	1947	Nolan Ryan
1980	Josh Kelley	1956	Johnny Rotten
1980	Wilmer Valderrama	1959	Anthony LaPaglia
		1969	Danny Moder
		1970	Minnie Driver
		1973	Portia de Rossi
		1977	Kerry Washington
		1981	Justin Timberlake

February 1   February 2

February 1		February 2	
1895	John Ford	1650	Nell Gwyn
1896	Anastasio Somoza Garcia	1745	Hannah More
1901	Clark Gable	1786	Harriette Wilson
1902	Langston Hughes	1859	Havelock Ellis
1918	Muriel Spark	1864	Margot Asquith
1931	Boris Yeltsin	1882	James Joyce
1939	Fritjof Capra	1886	Frank Lloyd
1965	Sherilyn Fenn	1901	Jascha Heifetz
1967	Laura Dern	1905	Ayn Rand
1968	Lisa Marie Presley	1923	Liz Smith
1975	Big Boi	1925	Elaine Stritch
1986	Lauren Conrad	1927	Stan Getz
1987	Heather Morris	1931	Judith Viorst
		1937	Tom Smothers
		1945	Isayas Afewerki

The Quotable Aquarius

		1947	Farrah Fawcett
		1954	Christie Brinkley
		1966	Robert DeLeo
		1969	Michael Sheen
		1970	Jennifer Westfeldt
		1977	Shakira

February 3

1809	Felix Mendelssohn
1811	Horace Greeley
1821	Elizabeth Blackwell
1826	Walter Bagehot
1874	Gertrude Stein
1894	Norman Rockwell
1907	James Michener
1909	Simone Weil
1939	Michael Cimino
1943	Blythe Danner
1948	Carlos Belo
1950	Morgan Fairchild
1956	Nathan Lane
1965	Maura Tierney
1970	Warwick Davis
1976	Isla Fisher
1990	Sean Kingston

February 4

1802	Mark Hopkins
1881	Fernand Léger
1902	Charles Lindbergh
1906	Dietrich Bonhoeffer
1913	Rosa Parks
1921	Betty Friedan
1947	Dan Quayle
1948	Alice Cooper
1962	Clint Black
1970	Gabrielle Anwar
1975	Natalie Imbruglia

February 5

1626	Madame de Sévigné
1837	D.L. Moody
1900	Adlai Stevenson
1914	William Burroughs
1919	Red Buttons
1928	Andrew Greeley

February 6

1756	Aaron Burr
1895	Babe Ruth
1911	Ronald Reagan
1917	Zsa Zsa Gabor
1939	Mike Farrell
1940	Tom Brokaw

1934	Hank Aaron	1945	Bob Marley
1948	Christopher Guest	1945	Michael Tucker
1948	Barbara Hershey	1950	Natalie Cole
1962	Jennifer Jason Leigh	1957	Kathy Najimy
1964	Laura Linney	1962	Axl Rose
1969	Bobby Brown	1973	Amy Robach
1987	Darren Criss	1985	Kris Humphries

February 7		February 8	
1478	Thomas More	1577	Robert Burton
1653	Arcangelo Corelli	1591	Guercino
1741	Henry Fuseli	1612	Samuel Butler
1812	Charles Dickens	1688	Emanuel Swedenborg
1832	Hannah Whitall Smith	1819	John Ruskin
1870	Alfred Adler	1828	Jules Verne
1883	Eubie Blake	1850	Kate Chopin
1885	Sinclair Lewis	1906	Chester Carlson
1932	Gay Talese	1911	Elizabeth Bishop
1960	James Spader	1921	Lana Turner
1962	Garth Brooks	1925	Jack Lemmon
1962	David Bryan	1931	James Dean
1965	Chris Rock	1940	Ted Koppel
1978	Ashton Kutcher	1941	Nick Nolte
		1953	Mary Steenburgen
		1955	John Grisham
		1968	Gary Coleman
		1969	Mary McCormack

February 9		February 10	
1737	Thomas Paine	1775	Charles Lamb
1773	William Henry Harrison	1890	Boris Pasternak
1874	Amy Lowell	1893	Jimmy Durante
1885	Alban Berg	1897	Judith Anderson

1891	Ronald Colman	1898	Bertolt Brecht
1902	Juanita Craft	1927	Leontyne Price
1914	Bill Veeck	1930	E.L. Konigsburg
1923	Brendan Behan	1930	Robert Wagner
1942	Carole King	1937	Roberta Flack
1943	Joe Pesci	1955	Greg Norman
1944	Alice Walker	1961	George Stephanopoulos
1945	Mia Farrow	1991	Emma Roberts
1963	Travis Tritt		
1979	Ziyi Zhang		

February 11		February 12	
1802	Lydia Child	1567	Thomas Campion
1847	Thomas Edison	1663	Cotton Mather
1907	William Levitt	1768	Francis II (France)
1909	Joseph Mankiewicz	1775	Louisa Adams
1916	Florynce Kennedy	1809	Charles Darwin
1917	Sidney Sheldon	1809	Abraham Lincoln
1926	Leslie Nielsen	1828	George Meredith
1936	Burt Reynolds	1880	John L. Lewis
1953	Jeb Bush	1881	Anna Pavlova
1961	Carey Lowell	1884	Max Beckmann
1962	Sheryl Crow	1893	Omar Bradley
1964	Sarah Palin	1915	Lorne Greene
1969	Jennifer Aniston	1934	Bill Russell
1979	Brandy	1938	Judy Blume
1992	Taylor Lautner	1942	Ehud Barak
		1952	Michael McDonald
		1958	Arsenio Hall
		1968	Josh Brolin
		1968	Chynna Phillips
		1980	Christina Ricci

February 13		February 14	
1885	Bess Truman	1818	Frederick Douglass
1910	Margaret Halsey	1894	Jack Benny
1919	Tennessee Ernie Ford	1902	Thelma Ritter
1923	Chuck Yeager	1913	Woody Hayes
1934	George Segal	1913	Jimmy Hoffa
1944	Stockard Channing	1921	Hugh Downs
1950	Donna Hanover	1934	Florence Henderson
1961	Henry Rollins	1942	Michael Bloomberg
1974	Robbie Williams	1946	Gregory Hines
1979	Mena Suvari	1972	Rob Thomas
		1992	Freddie Highmore

February 15		February 16	
1710	Louis XV (France)	1838	Henry Adams
1809	Cyrus McCormick	1926	John Schlesinger
1817	Charles Daubigny	1935	Sonny Bono
1820	Susan B. Anthony	1941	Kim Jong-il
1861	Alfred Whitehead	1948	Eckhart Tolle
1882	John Barrymore	1957	LeVar Burton
1899	Lillian Disney	1958	Ice-T
1899	Gale Sondergaard	1959	John McEnroe
1927	Harvey Korman		
1931	Claire Bloom		
1944	Mick Avory		
1947	Marisa Berenson		
1951	Jane Seymour		
1954	Matt Groening		
1986	Amber Riley		

February 17		February 18	
1843	Aaron Montgomery Ward	1848	Louis Tiffany
1874	Thomas Watson Sr.	1862	Charles Schwab
1877	Isabelle Eberhardt	1878	Martin Buber
1879	Dorothy Canfield Fisher	1883	Nikos Kazantzakis
1925	Hal Holbrook	1919	Jack Palance
1929	Chaim Potok	1922	Helen Gurley Brown
1934	Alan Bates	1925	George Kennedy
1938	Mary Frances Berry	1931	Johnny Hart
1945	Brenda Fricker	1931	Toni Morrison
1962	Lou Diamond Phillips	1932	Milos Forman
1963	Michael Jordan	1933	Yoko Ono
1963	Larry the Cable Guy	1934	Audre Lorde
1970	Dominic Purcell	1936	Jean Auel
1972	Billie Joe Armstrong	1948	Sinead Cusack
1972	Denise Richards	1950	Cybill Shepherd
1974	Jerry O'Connell	1954	John Travolta
1981	Paris Hilton	1957	Vanna White
1989	Chord Overstreet	1964	Matt Dillon
1991	Bonnie Wright	1965	Dr. Dre
		1968	Molly Ringwald

Talents

No one can arrive from being talented alone. God gives talent; work transforms talent into genius.
Dancer Anna Pavlova, born 2/12/1881

- **Individuality**
- **Freedom**
- **Intelligence**
- **Involvement in Social Issues**

- **Egalitarianism**
- **High Principles**
- **Vision**

Individuality

What's great is that there's no one way to dance. And that's kind of my philosophy about everything.
Ellen DeGeneres, born 1/28/1958

Aquarius is the sign of originality. Aquarians share general tendencies, but each of you develops your own brand of individuality. To Aquarius, unique behavior is desirable behavior. The novels of Aquarian Ayn Rand (2/2/1905) celebrate the triumphs of the individual over societal restrictions.

If a life could have a theme song—and I believe every worthwhile one has—mine is a religion, an obsession, a mania or all of these expressed in one word—individualism. I was born with that obsession, and I've never seen and do not know now a cause more worthy, more misunderstood, more seemingly hopeless, and tragically needed.

Ayn Rand, born 2/2/1905

There is no excellent beauty that hath not some strangeness in the proportion.

Francis Bacon, born 1/22/1561

The desire to be singular and to astonish by ways out of the common seems to me to be the source of many virtues.

Madame de Sévigné, born 2/5/1626

The boughs of no two trees ever have the same arrangement. Nature always produces individuals; she never produces classes.

Lydia Child, born 2/11/1802

The weakest among us has a gift, however seemingly trivial, which is peculiar to him and which worthily used will be a gift also to his race.

John Ruskin, born 2/8/1819

"The time has come," the Walrus said,
 "To talk of many things:
Of shoes—and ships—and sealing wax—
Of cabbages—and kings—
And why the sea is boiling hot—
 And whether pigs have wings."

Lewis Carroll, born 1/27/1832
The Walrus and the Carpenter

Philosophy is a purely personal matter. A genuine
philosopher's credo is the outcome of a single
complex personality; it cannot be transferred. No two
persons, if sincere, can have the same philosophy.

Havelock Ellis, born 2/2/1859

If they ask me in the next world, "Why were you not
Moses?" I will know the answer. But if they ask me,
"Why were you not Zusya?" I will have nothing to say.

Martin Buber, born 2/18/1878,
story about master Rabbi Zusya

Nobody can be exactly like me. Sometimes
even I have trouble doing it.

Tallulah Bankhead, born 1/31/1902

Freedom is the recognition that no single person, no single
authority of government has a monopoly on the truth, but that
every individual life is infinitely precious, that every one of us put
on this world has been put there for a reason and has something
to offer.

Ronald Reagan, born 2/6/1911

And she had nothing to fall back on; not maleness,
not whiteness, not ladyhood, not anything. And
out of the profound desolation of her reality
she may very well have invented herself.
Toni Morrison, born 2/18/1931

No person is your friend (or kin) who demands
your silence, or denies your right to grow and be
perceived as fully blossomed as you were intended.
Alice Walker, born 2/9/1944

My grandmother taught me to approach fashion
as creative therapy. It's my favorite outlet for self-
expression—I rarely wear anything the same way twice.
Marisa Berenson, born 2/15/1947

I realized that there is something wrong if you're always thinking
you're supposed to live your life to fit into some type of popular
consensus. Most people live their lives like that. They dress a
certain way because it's acceptable; they act a particular way
because they've been conditioned and domesticated. They've been
taught by reward and punishment what's going to be tolerated
and what is not. But I finally realized that this is my one and
only life. It's my obligation to be true to my soul, my being. So I
had to clear a space from all society's rules and admit who I was.
Ellen DeGeneres, born 1/26/1958

My style is difficult to emulate. It's pretty idiosyncratic.
John McEnroe, born 2/16/1959

Freedom

Aquarius insists upon personal freedom for all. Each person deserves the freedom to live and express themselves however they choose. President Abraham Lincoln (2/12/1809) officially abolished American slavery with the Emancipation Proclamation.

> *I do order and declare that ALL PERSONS HELD AS SLAVES within said designated States and parts of States ARE, AND HENCEFORWARD SHALL BE FREE!*
>
> Abraham Lincoln, born 2/12/1809
> Emancipation Proclamation

> *Here's freedom to him who would speak,*
> *Here's freedom to him who would write,*
> *For there's none ever feared*
> *that the truth should be heard,*
> *Except he who the truth would indict.*
>
> Robert Burns, born 1/25/1759

> *Yet, Freedom! yet thy banner, torn, but flying,*
> *Streams like the thunder-storm against the wind.*
>
> Lord Byron, born 1/22/1788
> Childe Harold's Pilgrimage

> *Fourscore and seven years ago our fathers brought forth on this continent a new nation, conceived in liberty, and dedicated to the proposition that all men are created equal . . . that we here highly resolve that these dead shall not have died in vain; that this nation, under God, shall have a new birth of freedom; and that government of the people, by the people, for the people, shall not perish from the earth.*
>
> Abraham Lincoln, born 2/12/1809
> Gettysburg Address

I only ask to be free. The butterflies are free.
Charles Dickens, born 2/7/1812

If you have the household keys, throw them in the
well and go away. Be free, be free as the wind.
Anton Chekhov, born 1/29/1860
The Cherry Orchard

There are two good things in life—freedom
of thought and freedom of action.
W. Somerset Maugham, born 1/25/1874
Of Human Bondage

We look forward to a world founded upon four essential human
freedoms. The first is freedom of speech and expression—
everywhere in the world. The second is freedom of every person
to worship God in his own way—everywhere in the world. The
third is freedom from want—everywhere in the world. The fourth
is freedom from fear—anywhere in the world.
Franklin Roosevelt, born 1/30/1882

Don't put no constrictions on da
people. Leave 'em ta hell alone.
Jimmy Durante, born 2/10/1893

There is no denying that the winds of freedom are blowing, east
and west. They are brisk and bracing winds, sweeping out the
old and, I believe, ushering in a new era of freedom, an era in
which democracy is once again recognized as the new ideal.
Ronald Reagan, born 2/6/1911

Freedom is like taking a bath: You
got to keep doing it every day.
Florynce Kennedy, born 2/11/1916

You are your own stories and therefore free to imagine and experience what it means to be human without wealth. What it feels like to be human without domination over others, without reckless arrogance, without fear of others unlike you, without rotating, rehearsing and reinventing the hatreds you learned in the sandbox. And although you don't have complete control over the narrative (no author does, I can tell you), you could nevertheless create it.

Toni Morrison, born 2/18/1931,
Commencement speech

I've always had my freedom. The price I paid for it was popularity and money.
Football legend Jim Brown, born 2/17/1936

I wanted the freedom to do what I wanted to do. And I wanted to do it my way.
Michael Jordan, born 2/17/1963

Snowboarding is free. You make up your own rules.
Hannah Teter, born 1/27/1987

Intelligence

The ancients assigned each zodiac sign to one of the four elements—Fire, Water, Air or Earth. Air claims visionary Aquarius, thoughtful Libra and talkative Gemini. The Air element enhances intellect, analysis, judgment and innovation. Aquarius is a thinking sign, curious about everything. You're quick, literate and inventive.

I have taken all knowledge to be my province.
Francis Bacon, born 1/22/1561

When I step into this library, I cannot
understand why I ever step out of it.
Madame de Sévigné, born 2/5/1626

I love to lose myself in other men's minds.
Charles Lamb, born 2/10/1775

Though the theory is worthless without the well-
observed facts, the facts are useless without
the frame of the theory to receive them.
Charles Darwin, born 2/12/1809

The brain can be developed just the same as the
muscles can be developed, if one will only take the
pains to train the mind to think. Why do so many men
never amount to anything? Because they don't think.
Thomas Edison, born 2/11/1847

I ransack public libraries, and find
them full of sunk treasure.
Virginia Woolf, born 1/25/1882

If devotion to truth is the hallmark of morality, then there is no
greater, nobler, more heroic form of devotion than the act of a
man who assumes the responsibility of thinking . . . Thinking is
man's only basic virtue, from which all the others proceed.
Ayn Rand, born 2/2/1905
Atlas Shrugged

Ben was an intellectual, and intellectuals, say what
you like, seemed to last longer than anyone else.
Muriel Spark, born 2/1/1918
The Father's Daughters

I go to different schools and pick up credits where I can, depending on where I'm working. It's good to do something else when you're caught up in this weird, fraudulent, hot-celebrity world that can be really silly.

Laura Dern, born 2/1/1967

Involvement in Social Issues

Aquarius is the only astrological sign symbolized by a figure in the act of helping others. As the zodiac was initially observed, the annual fertilizing Flood of the Nile occurred when the Aquarius constellation centered the night sky. Aquarius takes a strong stance on societal issues and gets actively involved in improving conditions.

Charles Dickens (2/7/1812) wrote about the lower classes. Artist Norman Rockwell (2/3/1894) addressed issues like segregation in his popular *Saturday Evening Post* covers. Aquarian Paul Newman (1/26/1925) parlayed his movie star status to a food company contributing profits to charity. The television shows of Oprah Winfrey (1/29/1954) brought difficult social issues into Middle American living rooms.

For justice, though she's painted blind,
Is to the weaker side inclined.

Samuel Butler, born 2/8/1612
Hudibras

When it shall be said in any country in the world, my poor are happy; neither ignorance nor distress is to be found among them; my jails are empty or prisoners, my streets of beggars; the aged are not in want, the taxes are not oppressive; the rational world is my friend, because I am a friend of its happiness—when these things can be said, then may that country boast of its constitution and its government.

Thomas Paine, born 2/9/1737

Man's inhumanity to man makes
countless thousands mourn.

Robert Burns, born 1/25/1759
Man Was Made to Mourn

I expose slavery in this country, because to expose
it is to kill it. Slavery is one of those moments of
darkness to whom the light of truth is death.

Frederick Douglass, born 2/14/1818

Cautious, careful people, always casting about to preserve their
reputation and social standing, never can bring about a reform.
Those who are really in earnest must be willing to be anything or
nothing in the world's estimation, and publicly and privately, in
season and out, avow their sympathies with despised ideas and
their advocates, and bear the consequences.

Susan B. Anthony, born 2/15/1820

The ages are but baubles hung upon
The thread of some strong lives—and one slight wrist
May lift a century above the dust.

Edith Wharton, born 1/24/1862
A Torchbearer, Artemis to Actaeon

Perhaps all this modern ferment of what's
known as "social conscience" or "civic
responsibility" isn't a result of the sense of
duty, but of the old, old craving for beauty.

Dorothy Canfield Fisher, born 2/17/1879
The Bent Twig

We boast of vast achievements and of power,
Of human progress knowing no defeat,
Of strange new marvels, every day and hour—
And here's the bread line in the wintry street!

Berton Braley, born 1/29/1882
The Bread Line

But life lived only for oneself does not truly satisfy men or women. There is a hunger in Americans today for larger purposes beyond the self. That is the reason for the religious revival and the new resonance of "family."

Betty Friedan, born 2/4/1921
The Second Stage

He told all us kids: "If you don't vote, I'll disown you." It was not an idle threat. He believed strongly that we should all take part in politics, at the very least by voting. He loved to argue about politics. I disagreed with him on some issues, and he relished thrashing it out.

Neil Newman about father Paul Newman, born 1/25/1926

Activism is my rent for living on this planet.

Alice Walker, born 2/9/1944

I believe real strongly in putting
something back into society.

Tom Selleck, born 1/29/1945

Get up, stand up
Stand up for your rights
Get up, stand up
Never give up the fight.

Bob Marley, born 2/6/1945

*I realize that I've been given many gifts, not
least of which is my ability to communicate on
behalf of people who don't have a voice.*
Jane Seymour, born 2/15/1951

*But for the past four years we've been leading the
way for doing issues that change people's lives.*
Oprah Winfrey, born 1/29/1954

*At age 50, you have to feel you're contributing to
something. If you don't I think you die a little bit.*
John Travolta, born 2/18/1954

*I'm ready for a change. The corporate work
is suddenly boring and unimportant, and I
want to do something to help people.*
John Grisham, born 2/8/1955
Street Lawyer

*I had a drive to help, an interest in government and
current events since I was a little kid, and I had become
aware of the impact of common sense public policy
during the presidency of Ronald Reagan (2/6/1911).*
Sarah Palin, born 2/11/1964

Aquarian Causes

Aquarius	Birthdate	Cause
Abraham Lincoln	2/12/1809	Abolition of slavery
Frederick Douglass	2/14/1818	Abolition of slavery
Susan B. Anthony	2/15/1820	Women's suffrage
Rosa Parks	2/4/1913	Desegregation
Betty Friedan	2/4/1921	Women's liberation
Helen Gurley Brown	2/18/1922	Sex and the Single Girl
Germaine Greer	1/29/1939	Women's liberation

| Angela Davis | 1/26/1944 | Civil rights |
| Oprah Winfrey | 1/29/1954 | Third world education |

Those who love a cause are those who love the
life which has to be led in order to serve it.
Simone Weil, born 2/3/1909

Women looked at themselves and their lives very
differently and were seen by society very differently
than they are today . . . Wife, mother, housewife—she
really wasn't supposed to be a person herself. That's
certainly not true now. And I helped make the change.
Betty Friedan, born 2/4/1921

Egalitarianism

Aquarius is the great leveler of the zodiac, the change agent who tears down existing structures to ensure an even playing field. You unequivocally accept that all are created equal and deserve equal opportunity. The mythological figure Prometheus is associated with Aquarius because of his service to humanity. Recognizing that fire could improve lives, Prometheus defied the gods by stealing their fire and sharing it with mankind.

Thy godlike crime was to be kind,
To render with thy precepts less
The sum of human wretchedness,
And strengthen man with his own mind.
But, baffled as thou wert from high,
Still, in thy patient energy,
In the endurance and repulse

Of thine impenetrable spirit,
Which earth and heaven could not convulse
A mighty lesson we inherit . . .

Lord Byron, born 1/22/1788
Prometheus

I believe in the equality of man; and I believe that
religious duties consist in doing justice, loving mercy,
and endeavoring to make our fellow-creatures happy.

Thomas Paine, born 2/9/1737
The Age of Reason

As a nation, we began by declaring that all men are created
equal. We now practically read it, all men are created equal
except Negroes. When the Know-nothings get control, it will
read, all men are created equal except Negroes and foreigners
and Catholics. When it comes to this I shall prefer emigrating
to some country where they make no pretense of loving liberty.

Abraham Lincoln, born 2/12/1809

I want to be something so much worthier
than the doll in the doll's house.

Charles Dickens, born 2/7/1812
Our Mutual Friend

I know of no rights of race superior
to the rights of humanity.

Frederick Douglass, born 2/14/1818

Join the union, girls, and together say,
"Equal Pay for Equal Work!"

Susan B. Anthony, born 2/15/1820

I would venture to guess that Anon, who wrote so many poems without signing them, was often a woman.

Virginia Woolf, born 1/25/1882

Ultimately a hero is a man who would argue with the Gods, and so awakens devils to contest his vision.

Norman Mailer, born 1/31/1923

They say we don't have the "mental necessities" to sit behind the desk, we just have God-given talent. But, man, I had to work hard, too. I had to think. I didn't have any more natural talent than Ted Williams or Joe DiMaggio. I played the game 23 years, and that tells me I had to study some pitchers pretty well. But no—I was a "dumb s.o.b." It's racism. These things really anger me.

Hank Aaron, born 2/5/1934

I don't care what your race or gender is. Bring your golf clubs and go play.

Jack Nicklaus, born 1/21/1940

I don't want my children to grow up thinking they are better than the rest of society. We're very much aware of our middle-class roots. We want to maintain those roots for the sake of the children.

Tom Brokaw, born 2/6/1940

I don't have prejudice against meself. My father was a white and my mother was black. Them call me half-caste or whatever. Me don't dip on nobody's side. Me don't dip on the black man's side nor the white man's side. Me dip on God's side, the one who create me and cause me to come from black and white.

Bob Marley, born 2/6/1945

There are so many women in their 40s and 50s who are still sexy and innovative and learning new things, whether it's taking classes or starting new careers. But in Hollywood, we're kind of thrown aside a lot, which is pretty pathetic. I wish women in this country would rise up and say, "No! We want to see women like us on TV again."

Morgan Fairchild, born 2/3/1950

Education is the most important gift you can give anyone, because giving an education begins to change a life forever. No child should have to go to a school where there is no running water. Every child should feel safe and secure. Every child should have access to books that inspire. Every child's love of learning should be supported and nurtured.

Oprah Winfrey, born 1/29/1954

I do love to shop for products in other countries—you get a sense of what beauty means in a different society.

Actress Kerry Washington, born 1/31/1977

Aquarius Specialty: Breaking Traditional Barriers

Aquarians insist upon equal opportunity for all. Many Aquarians have overthrown existing order by breaking through traditional barriers.

- Heeding his conscience over popular and political opinion, Abraham Lincoln (2/12/1809) formally abolished slavery in the United States
- Charles Darwin (2/12/1809) refused to put the Bible above science as he developed his theory of evolution
- Elizabeth Blackwell (2/3/1821) was the first female doctor in the United States. Jane Seymour (2/15/1951) played a similar role in the TV series *Dr. Quinn, Medicine Woman*

- Charles Lindbergh (2/4/1902) was first person to fly across the Atlantic Ocean
- Rosa Parks (2/4/1913) accelerated desegregation by refusing to surrender her seat on a crowded bus
- Jackie Robinson (1/31/1919) broke professional baseball's color barrier
- Boston Celtic Bill Russell (2/12/1934) was the first African-American coach of a major U.S. sports team
- Burt Reynolds (2/11/1936) became mass media's first male centerfold
- Farrah Fawcett (2/2/1947) posed nude for *Playboy* at age 50
- *Glee*'s Amber Riley (2/15/1986) demonstrates that plus-size can be popular and successful

The Devil under form of Baboon is our grandfather.
Charles Darwin, born 2/12/1809

She was twelve years old when she told Eddie Willers that she would run the railroad when they grew up. She was fifteen when it occurred to her for the first time that women did not run railroads and that people might object. To hell with that, she thought—and never worried about it again.
Ayn Rand, born 2/2/1905
Atlas Shrugged

The first female pope. I'd allow priests to marry and women to become priests. And I'd have a lot more singing and dancing going on.
Florence Henderson, born 2/14/1934,
about career plans for her next life

Today, a couple of women I met in the store said,
"Thank you for what you're doing." That's just
different than, "I liked you in Beetle Juice."
Geena Davis, born 1/21/1956,
about her TV role as U.S. President

High Principles

Tradition divides zodiac signs into three types of action—Cardinal (dynamic), Fixed (purposeful) and Mutable (adaptable). Fixed signs Aquarius, Taurus, Leo and Scorpio are characterized by a determined adherence to principles. Taurus clings to those axioms that ensure personal security; Leo heroically insists on doing the right thing. Aquarius honors those values that improve the human condition.

I love the man that can smile in trouble, that can gather strength from distress, and grow brave by reflection. 'Tis the business of little minds to shrink, but he whose heart is firm, and whose conscience approves his conduct, will pursue his principles unto death.
Thomas Paine, born 2/9/1737

Be sure to put your feet in the right place. Then stand firm.
Abraham Lincoln, born 2/12/1809

Really decent people are only to be found amongst men who have definite, either conservative or radical, convictions; so-called moderate men are much inclined to rewards, commissions, orders, promotions.
Anton Chekhov, born 1/29/1860

*Art, if it is to be reckoned as one of the great
values of life, must teach men humility,
tolerance, wisdom and magnanimity. The
value of art is not beauty, but right action.*
W. Somerset Maugham, born 1/25/1874

*Nobody grows old by merely living a number of years.
People grow old by deserting their ideals. Years may
wrinkle the skin, but to give up wrinkles the soul.*
Douglas MacArthur, born 1/26/1880

Rules are not necessarily sacred, principles are.
Franklin Roosevelt, born 1/30/1882

*Men who have offered their lives for their country know that
patriotism is not the fear of something; it is the love of something.
Patriotism with us is not the hatred of Russia; it is the love of this
republic and of the ideal of liberty of man and mind in which it
was born, and to which this Republic is dedicated.*
Adlai Stevenson, born 2/5/1900

*The spread of evil is the symptom of a vacuum.
Whenever evil wins, it is only by default: by the
moral failure of those who evade the fact that
there can be no compromise on basic principles.*
Ayn Rand, born 2/2/1905
Capitalism: The Unknown Ideal

Vision

Astrologers assign rulership of Aquarius to Uranus, god of the
heavens. Aquarius supplies the vision. *Utopia* by Thomas More
(2/7/1478) describes education, employment and religion within the
perfect society. *Common Sense* by Thomas Paine (2/9/1737) pictures

the strengths of the American colonies once freed from England. Both Aquarian works were among the most influential publications of their time and beyond.

In Utopia, where every man has a right to everything, they all know that if care is taken to keep the public stores full, no private man can want anything; for among them there is no unequal distribution, so that no man is poor, none in necessity; and though no man has anything, yet they are all rich; for what can make a man so rich as to lead a serene and cheerful life, free from anxieties.

Thomas More, born 2/7/1478
Utopia

Freedom has been hunted around the globe; reason was considered as rebellion; and the slavery of fear made men afraid to think. But such is the irresistible nature of truth that all it asks, all it wants, is the liberty of appearing. In such a situation, man becomes what he ought to be.

Thomas Paine, born 2/9/1737
Common Sense

If we can know where we are and something about how we got there, we might see where we are trending, and if the outcomes which lie naturally in our course are unacceptable, make timely change.

Abraham Lincoln, born 2/12/1809

Dream lofty dreams, and as you dream, so shall you become. Your vision is the promise of what you shall at last unveil.

John Ruskin, born 2/8/1819

The Quotable Aquarius

*The greatest thing a human being ever does in
this world is to see something . . . To see clearly
is poetry, prophecy and religion, all in one.*
John Ruskin, born 2/8/1819

*True originality consists not in a new
manner but in a new vision.*
Edith Wharton, born 1/24/1862

*I knew I had no lyrical quality, a small vocabulary, little gift of
metaphor. The original and striking simile never occurred to me.
Poetic flights . . . were beyond my powers. On the other hand, I
had an acute power of observation, and it seemed to me that I
could see a great many things that other people missed. I could
put down in clear terms what I saw . . . I knew that I should never
write as well as I could wish, but I thought, with pains, that I
could arrive at writing as well as my natural defects allowed.*
W. Somerset Maugham, born 1/25/1874

*I unconsciously decided that if it wasn't
an ideal world, it should be.*
Norman Rockwell, born 2/3/1894

I want people to have the grandest vision for their lives.
Oprah Winfrey, born 1/29/1954

*I think if we were all to be honest with ourselves, we would agree
that rather than dealing with the reality of things, we've kind of
allowed ourselves to become a distracted people and invested in
crazy kinds of things like reality-TV shows and tabloidism. We've
kept ourselves busy at a time when it would really have benefited
us to be awake and be involved in our future and our legacy.*
Singer Sheryl Crow, born 2/11/1962

The Quotable Aquarius

Double-Edged Traits

The good things of life are not to be had
single, but come to us with a mixture.

Charles Lamb, born 2/10/1775

- **Mental Activity**
- **Superstition**
- **Independence**
- **Objectivity**

- **Rebelliousness**
- **Unpredictability**
- **Abrupt Changes**

Mental Activity

He's very clever, but sometimes
his brains go to his head.

Margot Asquith, born 2/2/1864

Aquarian intellect ranges up to the genius level—consider Mozart, Edison, Oprah, Timberlake. You're always thinking. Your active mind turns information into solutions but also churns along the repetitive wheels of overthinking. Absorption in your own thoughts can leave you distracted, absentminded and out of touch with the reality at hand.

Read not to contradict and confute, nor to
believe and take for granted, nor to find talk
and discourse, but to weigh and consider.
Francis Bacon, born 1/22/1561

We may some day catch an abstract
truth by the tail, and then we shall have
our religion and our immortality.
Henry Adams, born 2/16/1838

The power to love what is purely
abstract is given to few.
Margot Asquith, born 2/2/1864
More or Less About Myself

It takes a lot of time to be a genius, you have to sit
around so much doing nothing, really doing nothing.
Gertrude Stein, born 2/3/1874
Everybody's Autobiography

Energy is the power that drives every human
being. It is not lost by exertion but maintained
by it, for it is a faculty of the psyche.
Germaine Greer, born 1/29/1939

The greatest discovery of all time is that a person can
change his future by merely changing his attitude.
Oprah Winfrey, born 1/29/1954

I think you should learn, of course, and some days you must learn a great deal. But you should also have days when you allow what is already in you to swell up inside of you until it touches everything. And you can feel it inside you. If you never take time out to let that happen, then you just accumulate facts, and they begin to rattle around inside of you. You can make noise with them, but never really feel anything with them. It's hollow.

E.L. Konigsburg, born 2/10/1930
From the Mixed-Up Files of Mrs. Basil E. Frankweiler

The mind is a superb instrument if used rightly. Used wrongly, however, it becomes very destructive. To put it more accurately, it is not so much that you use your mind wrongly—you usually don't use it at all. It uses you. This is the disease. You believe that you are your mind. This is the delusion. The instrument has taken you over.

Eckhart Tolle, born 2/16/1948

It is sometimes best to slip over thoughts and not go to the bottom of them.

Madame de Sévigné, born 2/5/1626

Nothing seems to me so inane as bookish language in conversation.

Stendhal, born 1/23/1783

Of its own beauty is the mind diseased.

Lord Byron, born 1/22/1788
Childe Harold's Pilgrimage

Too much brilliance has its disadvantages, and misplaced wit may raise a laugh, but often beheads a topic of profound interest.

Margot Asquith, born 2/2/1864

*If things happen all the time you are never nervous. It
is when they are not happening that you are nervous.*
Gertrude Stein, born 2/3/1874

*If any part of your uncertainty is a conflict between
your heart and your mind, follow your mind.*
Ayn Rand, born 2/2/1905

*You can't dance if you've got too
much muck in your head.*
Yoko Ono, born 2/18/1933

Our feelings are our most genuine paths to knowledge.
Audre Lorde, born 2/18/1934

When the customer says yes, stop talking.
Mayor Michael Bloomberg, born 2/14/1942

*I'd like to be more patient! I just want everything now. I've tried
to meditate, but it's really hard for me to stay still. I'd like to try
to force myself to do it, because everybody says how wonderful
meditation is for you, but I can't shut my mind up. So patience
and learning how to do nothing is key.*
Ellen DeGeneres, born 1/28/1958

I think too much, but otherwise, I'm happy.
Jennifer Aniston, born 2/11/1969

Superstition

With greater incidence than other zodiac signs, Aquarians
resort to quirky superstitions. (Several famous Aquarians make a
point of claiming no superstitions at all.) Superstitious observations
may smooth your path, but they use up valuable time and allow the
outside world to dismiss you as eccentric.

There is a superstition in avoiding superstition.
Francis Bacon, born 1/22/1561

*I had only one superstition. I made sure to
touch all the bases when I hit a home run.*
Babe Ruth, born 2/6/1895

*Superstition is foolish, childish, primitive
and irrational—but how much does
it cost you to knock on wood?*
Judith Viorst, born 2/2/1931

It is far harder to kill a phantom than a reality.
Virginia Woolf, born 1/25/1882

*I have a fit if someone brings peanuts
backstage or whistles backstage.*
Singer Ruth Brown, born 1/30/1928

*The golfing gods think you're going to move
it, so fool them and leave it where it is.*
Greg Norman, born 2/10/1955,
about changing the date for a frequently rained-out event

*I got three goals that night, and after
that you couldn't have torn that number
off me. Not that I'm superstitious.*
Wayne Gretzky, born 1/26/1961,
about his unusual number 99

*It's good to know you're not in control of
everything. Superstitions tell you that.*
George Stephanopoulos, born 2/10/1961

Aquarius Specialty: Superstitions

- Paris Hilton (2/17/1981) knocks on wood when someone predicts something she doesn't want to happen

- Actor Christian Bale (1/30/1974) laughs at superstition and chooses to walk under ladders rather than avoiding them

- Hockey's Bruce Gardiner (2/11/1971) broke long scoring droughts by dipping his hockey sticks in toilets

- When Michael Jordan (2/17/1963) returned from "retirement," he took the number 45 instead of his retired number 23. Things just weren't the same. Jordan soon returned to wearing his old number and regained his earlier basketball form.

- To channel his college success, Michael Jordan (2/17/1963) wore University of North Carolina shorts under his larger Bulls shorts

- Axl Rose (2/6/1962) of Guns N' Roses won't give a concert in any city that begins with the letter "M" because he believes that the letter is cursed

- Hockey legend Wayne Gretzky (1/26/1961) always tucked the right side of his hockey jersey into his pants

- Mia Farrow (2/9/1945) carries a marble for good luck

- Along with cash, the Boston Red Sox acquired the Curse of the Bambino when they traded Babe Ruth (2/6/1895) to the New York Yankees. After winning 5 of the first 15 World Series, Boston spent the next 86 years in a championship drought. The Yankees, on the other hand, earned a record 26 World Series titles over that same period.

Independence

Sagittarians and Aquarians require independence. Skittish Sagittarius needs to feel personally unrestrained, so Sagittarius frames commitments as loosely as possible. Aquarius demands the right of refusal to conform. Aquarian independence helps you develop your individuality, but your insistence on a separate space can leave you lonely and removed from the mainstream.

Independence is happiness.
Susan B. Anthony, born 2/15/1820

Let me listen to me and not to them.
Gertrude Stein, born 2/3/1874

A woman must have money and a room
of her own if she is to write fiction.
Virginia Woolf, born 1/25/1882
A Room of One's Own

I need no warrant for being, and no word of sanction
upon my being. I am the warrant and the sanction.
Ayn Rand, born 2/2/1905
Anthem

Most women still need a room of their own and the
only way to find it may be outside their own homes.
Germaine Greer, born 1/29/1939
The Female Eunuch

The only person swinging your clubs was you, not your coach . . . I realized that to achieve the kind of independence I would need to be successful, it was up to me to truly understand the game's cause and effect, alone and unaided. Since then, I've tried never to rely on someone else.

Jack Nicklaus, born 1/21/1940

In search of my mother's garden, I found my own.
Alice Walker, born 2/9/1944

You just need enough money to say no.
Cybill Shepherd, born 2/18/1950

You cannot let other people define your life for
you. You are the author of your own life.
Oprah Winfrey, born 1/29/1954

But I, ever the independent, was proudly GDI.
Sarah Palin, born 2/11/1964,
about her college years

And that was what now she often felt the need of—to think; well,
not even to think. To be silent; to be alone. All the being and the
doing, expansive, glittering, vocal, evaporated; and one shrunk
with a sense of solemnity, to being oneself . . . When life sank
down for a moment, the range of experience seemed limitless.
Virginia Woolf, born 1/25/1882
To the Lighthouse

I think there is a magic in giving things up. There
is a magic in being willing to let go of something
that has been your identity. I let go of my identity
completely, and it was so freeing and lovely.
Alice Walker, born 2/9/1944,
about giving up writing

One can acquire everything in
solitude—except character.
Stendhal, born 1/23/1783

There are days when solitude, for someone my age, is
a heady wine that intoxicates you with freedom, others
when it is a bitter tonic, and still others when it is a
poison that makes you beat your head against the wall.

Colette, born 1/28/1873
Earthly Paradise

I will not serve that in which I no longer believe,
whether it call itself my home, my fatherland,
or my church: and I will try to express myself in
some mode of life or art as freely as I can.

James Joyce, born 2/2/1882
A Portrait of the Artist as a Young Man

Fame always brings loneliness. Success is as
ice cold and lonely as the north pole.

Writer Vicki Baum, born 1/24/1888

What's wrong with dropping out? To me, this is
the whole point: one's right to withdraw from
a social environment that offers no spiritual
sustenance, and to mind one's own business.

William Burroughs, born 2/5/1914

Some people are not gonna get the nice side
of me all the time, but that's just too bad
'cause I'm not gonna pretend anymore. I'm
not gonna sacrifice my spirit for nobody.

Alicia Keys, born 1/25/1981

Objectivity

The Water-Bearer's vantage point in the skies lends the objectivity that allows broad vision. You're insightful, quick to see how the pieces fit together, skilled at anticipating where attention should focus next. But your Aquarian remoteness keeps others at arm's length and allows you to disengage from reality. Some Aquarians thrive on the stage because you feel part of a crowd while still maintaining a detached perspective.

We're harmless megalomaniacs, fanatic in our devotion to a profession which rarely rewards us with a livelihood. Since we court public display we're the foes of privacy. The glass house is our favorite residence.

Tallulah Bankhead, born 1/31/1902

Once you get on stage, everything is right. I feel the most beautiful, complete, fulfilled. I think that's why, in the case of noncompromising career women, parts of our personal lives don't work out. One person can't give you the feeling that thousands of people give you.

Leontyne Price, born 2/10/1927

I'm a very shy person. The stage is the only place where I feel uninhibited. The audience becomes like a huge mirror in which I look at my feelings reflected and they respond to me. We become like one. That's the magic of a good performance.

Shakira, born 2/2/1977

They chose me to be Dorothy. I was terrified to get on the stage. When I did I felt free!

Alicia Keys, born 1/25/1981,
about her first performing role, in kindergarten

He liked to observe emotions; they were like
red lanterns strung along the dark unknown of
another's personality, marking vulnerable points.

Ayn Rand, born 2/2/1905
Atlas Shrugged

Attachment is the great fabricator of illusions; reality
can be attained only by someone who is detached.

Simone Weil, born 2/3/1909

I always considered myself more well-rounded than most tennis
players: I read, I thought, I looked at the outside world. But I
always looked at it from a distance . . . In a lot of ways, I was
really oblivious to the outside world. And let me tell you: Once
you get away from the real world, it's very difficult to make that
transition back into it.

John McEnroe, born 2/16/1959

Every time a man unburdens his heart to a stranger
he reaffirms the love that unites humanity.

Germaine Greer, born 1/29/1939

Rebelliousness

The devil is strong in me . . . Rebellion is in the blood,
somehow or other. I can't go on without a fight.

Henry Adams, born 2/16/1838

You travel to your own beat. Aquarius refuses to accept what society defines as proper behavior. Actors James Dean (2/8/1931) and John Travolta (2/18/1954) bridged generations with their on-screen portrayals of youthful rebels. Rosa Parks (2/4/1913) accelerated desegregation when she refused to surrender her seat to a white bus rider. Baseball player Babe Ruth (2/6/1895) faced frequent suspension for flagrantly breaking team and league rules. Your rebellious attitude encourages reform but also alienates others while distracting from the issues.

I didn't get on the bus to get arrested.
I got on the bus to go home.
Rosa Parks, born 2/4/1913

If Rosa Parks had taken a poll before she sat down
in the bus in Montgomery, she'd still be standing.
Mary Frances Berry, born 2/17/1938

We should not be limited by what our society says.
Cybill Shepherd, born 2/18/1950

If you don't like it, lump it.
Charles Dickens, born 2/7/1812
Our Mutual Friend

There ain't no rules around here! We're
trying to accomplish something!
Thomas Edison, born 2/11/1847

Traditions that have lost their meaning
are the hardest of all to destroy.
Edith Wharton, born 1/24/1862

All progress had resulted from people
who took unpopular positions.
Adlai Stevenson, born 2/5/1900

Most of the men or women who have contributed
to our civilization or our culture have been vilified
in their day . . . As we denounce the rebellious,

the nonconformists, so we reward mediocrity
so long as it mirrors herd standards.

Tallulah Bankhead, born 1/31/1902

He felt a sudden spurt of rebellion, a need to recapture
and defiantly to reassert his own view of existence.

Ayn Rand, born 2/2/1905
Atlas Shrugged

You've got to rattle your cage door. You've got to let
them know that you're in there, and that you want
out. Make noise. Cause trouble. You may not win
right away, but you'll sure have a lot more fun.

Activist Florynce Kennedy, born 2/11/1916

Most writers who are timid are afraid of pissing people off,
because they feel they'll lose part of their audience. My feeling
had always been that one mustn't be afraid of that. It's much
better to write with the notion that if you're good enough, you
can change people's lives. That's one of the powerful motives of
writing, to feel that you've enlarged other people's consciousness.
And the way you do that is you open their minds. Now, that can
be painful and irritating and annoying or worse for people, but
you can't look back.

Norman Mailer, born 1/31/1923

But you can't show some far off idyllic conception
of behavior if you want the kids to come and see
the picture. You've got to show what it's really like,
and try to reach them on their own grounds.

James Dean, born 2/8/1931

Then Again, Maybe I Won't.
Book title by Judy Blume, born 2/12/1938

But I was a kind of performer, and my performances—my televised outbursts—broke through the clutter and drone of canned television tennis coverage. I had anger, presence, integrity. I was a rebel. And I was famous.

John McEnroe, born 2/16/1959

I hated high school, so I wore a fake black leather dress. It was a big "F—k you! I can't wait to get out of here!" I just looked like an idiot. We all do silly things in high school.

Singer Sarah McLachlan, born 1/28/1968

I'm still looking for trouble. I'm still disruptive. I'm still doing some things that other people don't like. I hear, "You're a moron," about once a day from someone in a genuine way—not as a joke. I see it, and I read it. I don't have anything that's too sacred to make fun of.

Ashton Kutcher, born 2/7/1978

Unpredictability

You keep yourself interested by staying unpredictable. You don't know what you'll do next, so life planning presents a challenge. The Aquarian path can unfold through a series of apparent accidents.

Let them cant about decorum
Who have characters to lose.

Robert Burns, born 1/25/1759
The Jolly Beggars

My policy is to have no policy.

Abraham Lincoln, born 2/12/1809,
as the Civil War began

Outwardly she differed from the rest of the teaching staff in that she was still in a state of fluctuating development, whereas they had only too understandably not trusted themselves to change their minds, particularly on ethical questions, after the age of twenty.

Muriel Spark, born 2/1/1918
The Prime of Miss Jean Brodie

What I like is when life wiggles its hips and throws me a surprise. All the experts said we couldn't produce these foods without chemical preservatives; they said we couldn't use fresh garlic and onions; they said we had to advertise; they said no business in the world could give away 100 percent of its profits. Well, we didn't listen to any of 'em, and just look at us.

Paul Newman, born 1/26/1925

Expect nothing. Live frugally on surprise.

Alice Walker, born 2/9/1944

I don't try to edit myself. I really do try to be that spontaneous and that free so that the audience doesn't know what's going to happen.

Ellen DeGeneres, born 1/28/1958,
about the secret to her success

He wanted me to be in exactly the right place all the time, which is exactly the wrong place for me. I go where the puck is going, not where it was. The thing that makes hockey great is the zillions of possibilities in every game. To play it well, you need room to improvise. To make me play in a certain spot in a certain time was like taking one of my skates off.

Wayne Gretzky, born 1/26/1961

Here I am—a California girl playing a New York City cop. I always say, "Don't put me in a box, sweetheart."
Mariska Hargitay, born 1/23/1964

I have a kid who sometimes thinks it's a good idea for us to jump in the pool with all our clothes on. Who am I to disagree with that?
Mariska Hargitay, born 1/23/1964

There is no security on this earth. Only opportunity.
Douglas MacArthur, born 1/26/1880

My life has been a series of crises.
Actress Lana Turner, born 2/8/1921

If we ever have a plan, we're screwed!
Paul Newman, born 1/26/1925

Just when I think I have learned the way to live, life changes.
Hugh Prather, born 1/23/1938

There is no such thing as security. There never has been.
Germaine Greer, born 1/29/1939

Rick was leaving, running away from the lease on the condo and the rented furniture therein, fleeing Cleveland and the Browns and their awful fans, scampering away to somewhere. He wasn't quite sure where . . . Wisely, he had signed only a six-month lease on the condo. Since college he'd lived a life of short leases and rented furniture and learned not to accumulate too many things.
John Grisham, born 2/8/1955
Playing for Pizza

*I would like to think that I'm somewhat
unpredictable and honest.*

John McEnroe, born 2/16/1959

*I definitely love my braids—they make me feel regal and
individualistic. But I'm a person who doesn't like to be stuck in
one style. So when I started feeling like I was getting stuck by
constantly wearing them, I did want to change it up a little.
That's when I started turning into a butterfly and making
changes. Mystery—this is the theme. Mysterious.*

Alicia Keys, born 1/25/1981

*Resolutions are like rules. They're
just made to be broken.*

Justin Timberlake, born 1/31/1981

*My sister is teaching me to cook. But you know,
it's not working out so well so far. I've burned
myself a couple of times here and there.*

Actress Heather Morris, born 2/1/1987

*I've been in, like, 5,000 accidents . . . and
I'm not even texting and driving.*

Heather Morris, born 2/1/1987

*If I had eight hours to chop down a tree,
I'd spend six sharpening my axe.*

Abraham Lincoln, born 2/12/1809

Abrupt Changes

Both Greek and Christian traditions tell of the great deluge sent from the heavens to eliminate an increasingly evil population. Noah and Deucalion and their spouses survive the floods so that new societies can develop. The Water-Bearer achieves social progress through violent, disruptive change. Old systems fall so that better systems can emerge.

On the personal level, Aquarius evolves through sudden transition. You leave previous circumstances far behind when you advance to a new level. Your transitions allow you to grow, but most people don't change as quickly as you do. Your abrupt conversions leave others bewildered, dazed and hurt.

> *We have it in our power to begin the world over*
> *again. A situation, similar to the present, hath*
> *not happened since the days of Noah until now.*
> *The birthday of a new world is at hand.*
> Thomas Paine, born 2/9/1737
> Common Sense

> *The dogmas of the quiet past are inadequate to*
> *the stormy present. As our case is new, so we must*
> *think anew and act anew. We must disenthrall*
> *ourselves, and then we shall save our country.*
> Abraham Lincoln, born 2/12/1809

> *The major advances in civilization are processes which*
> *all but wreck the societies in which they occur.*
> Alfred Whitehead, born 2/15/1861

Wars and revolutions, kings and Robespierres, are history's organic agents, its yeast. But revolutions are made by fanatical men of action with one-track minds, geniuses in their ability to

*confine themselves to a limited field. They overturn the old order
in a few hours or days, the whole upheaval takes a few weeks or
at most years, but the fanatical spirit that inspired the upheavals
is worshipped for decades thereafter, for centuries.*
Boris Pasternak, born 2/10/1890
Doctor Zhivago

*The sixties [start of Age of Aquarius] were characterized
by a heady belief in instantaneous solutions.*
Audre Lorde, born 2/18/1934

The keen spirit seizes the prompt occasion.
Hannah More, born 2/2/1745

*We cannot remain consistent with the world save
by growing inconsistent with our past selves.*
Havelock Ellis, born 2/2/1859

*Everybody knows if you are too careful you
are so occupied in being careful that you
are sure to stumble over something.*
Gertrude Stein, born 2/3/1874

*What I like, or one of the things I like, about motoring is the sense
it gives one of lighting accidentally, like a voyager who touches
another planet with the tip of his toe, upon scenes which would
have gone on, have always gone on, will go on, unrecorded, save
for this chance glimpse. Then it seems to me I am allowed to see
the heart of the world uncovered for a moment.*
Virginia Woolf, born 1/25/1882

The most wonderful accident that ever
happened to me was my coming out to this
God-given, vital, youthful, sunny place.
John Barrymore, born 2/15/1882,
about moving to Hollywood

To awaken quite alone in a strange town is
one of the most pleasant sensations in the
world. You are surrounded by adventure.
Freya Stark, born 1/31/1893

If there are obstacles, the shortest line between
two points may be the crooked line.
Bertolt Brecht, born 2/10/1898

When it comes to busting for that opening it's all
largely instinct. You've got a split second to decide.
You are right or you are wrong. You can't wait.
Jockey Eddie Arcaro, born 2/19/1916

People tell you to take this or that job because "it's
going to be your big break," but for me, the biggest
breaks were never the ones anyone planned.
Matt Dillon, born 2/18/1964

I've been on Oprah twice in six months, and 60
Minutes is calling. It's beyond my wildest dreams.
Chris Rock, born 2/7/1965

Mr. Phornish amiably growled, in his philosophical but not lucid
manner, that there was ups you see, and there was downs. It was
in vain to ask why ups, why downs; there they was, you know.
He had heerd it given for a truth that accordin' as the world
went round, which round it did rewolve undoubted, even the best

of gentlemen must take his turn of standing with his ed upside down and all his air a flying the wrong way into what you might call Space.

Charles Dickens, born 2/7/1812
Little Dorrit

My career has been like a heart-attack victim's. I was down at the bottom of the cellar and came back to the top. Now, with The Longest Yard, this picture's like the Deliverance of this period, of my life. I'll either come out of it looking like the old man of the century, or I'll come out of it with a pop.

Burt Reynolds, born 2/11/1936

I just fly along, and every now and then I get this "rediscovered" thing thrown at me. But I'm delighted that everybody thinks I'm going in the right direction.

Actress Stockard Channing, born 2/13/1944

History is an illogical record. It hinges on nothing. It is a story that changes and has accidents and recovers with scars.

Gretel Ehrlich, born 1/21/1946
Heart Mountain

A New York scout for a Hollywood production company saw The Firm in its original manuscript form, and suddenly there was a deal with Paramount. This happened before there was a publishing contract . . . Looking back, the movie deal has been the luckiest break of my career, and I knew nothing about it until it was nearly over.

John Grisham, born 2/8/1955

My soul kept me awake most of the night. Did I have the guts to walk away? Was I seriously considering taking a job which paid so little? I was literally saying good-bye to millions . . . The timing wasn't bad. With the marriage over, it somehow seemed fitting that I make drastic changes on all fronts.

John Grisham, born 2/8/1955
Street Lawyer

I like to move. I like change. I like architecture. Just when I think I like a contemporary house, I change to a Spanish-style house or a traditional.

Ellen DeGeneres, born 1/28/1958

The best laid schemes o' mice an' men
 Gang aft a-gley,
An' lea'e us nought but grief an' pain
 For promis'd joy.

Robert Burns, born 1/25/1759

I awoke one morning and found myself famous.

Lord Byron, born 1/22/1788,
on the immediate success of Childe Harold's Pilgrimage

After that season I could tell my life had changed forever. It's funny, you live for twenty years being able to walk down the street, then one day you wake up and you can't do it anymore.

Wayne Gretzky, born 1/26/1961

Aquarius Specialty: Sudden Life Changes

- The transatlantic flight of Charles Lindbergh (2/4/1902) brought instant fame and the tragic kidnapping of his young son

- High schooler Lana Turner (2/8/1921) skipped class to go to the soda fountain, only to be "discovered" and invited to star in the movies

- Boris Yeltsin (2/1/1931) abruptly resigned from the Russian Presidency

- Ballet dancer Mikhail Baryshnikov (1/27/1948) decided to defect from Russia just two days before sprinting away to a waiting car

- Actress Geena Davis (1/21/1956) devoted a year to Olympic-caliber archery

- Brett Butler (1/30/1958) went from television sitcom star to homeless

- Without warning, Keith Olbermann (1/27/1959) discontinued his daily MSNBC television program

- Basketball MVP Michael Jordan (2/17/1963) changed sports to pro baseball

- Sarah Palin (2/11/1964) resigned the governorship of Alaska in the middle of a term

- Gymnast Mary Lou Retton (1/24/1968) went from unknown to celebrity after vaulting to Olympic Gold

The Quotable Aquarius

Challenges

- Distance
- Temper
- Extreme Behavior
- Boredom
- Bluntness

Distance

Interaction with Aquarians can be cool and personal. You keep your distance. Famous Aquarians known for their interpersonal detachment include Thomas Edison (2/11/1847), James Joyce (2/2/1881) and Ronald Reagan (2/6/1911).

Secret, and self-contained, and solitary as an oyster.
Charles Dickens, born 2/7/1812

The true secret of giving advice is, after
you have honestly given it, to be perfectly
indifferent whether it is taken or not, and
never persist in trying to set people right.

Hannah Whitall Smith, born 2/7/1832

He was outcast from life's feast.

James Joyce, born 2/2/1882
A Painful Case

I don't remember anybody's name. How do
you think the "dahling" thing got started?

Zsa Zsa Gabor, born 2/6/1917

Here's a Quarter (Call Someone Who Cares)

Song title from Travis Tritt, born 2/9/1963

You want to know how it's really changed me? It's
filled me with regret for all those years when friends
were nominated for awards and I never called. Now
I know how wonderful it feels to get those calls.

Matt Dillon, born 2/18/1964,
about his nomination for an Oscar

I don't have any friends. I can't really have any friends. It's sad,
really. It's lonely. But that's how I am. That's why I say that I
don't really care what people think or say about me, because I'm
my own man. Nobody helps me, comes and pays my bills when
it's time [for them] to be paid, and nobody wakes me up in the
morning or works out for me.

Randy Moss, born 2/13/1977

Temper

Aquarius can explode with the most spectacular temper of the zodiac. You shift from focus to frenzy at a moment's provocation. Aquarian John McEnroe (2/16/1959) littered tennis tournaments with a series of memorable tantrums.

Anger makes dull men witty, but it keeps them poor.
Francis Bacon, born 1/22/1561

*The Queen was in a furious passion, and went
stomping about, and shouting, "Off with his head!"
or "Off with her head!" about once in a minute.*
Lewis Carroll, born 1/27/1832
Alice in Wonderland

I always throw my golf club in the direction I'm going.
President Ronald Reagan, born 2/6/1911

For one wild and rage-crazed minute I thought, "What a glorious, cleansing thing it would be to let go." To hell with the image of the patient black freak I was supposed to create. I could throw down my bat, stride over to the Phillies dugout, grab one of those white sons of bitches and smash his teeth in with my despised black fist.
Baseball player Jackie Robinson, born 1/31/1919,
who never surrendered to temper

*Anger stirs and wakes in her; it opens its mouth, and
like a hot-mouthed puppy, laps up the dredges of her
shame. Anger is better. There is a sense of being in
anger. A reality and presence. An awareness of worth.*
Toni Morrison, born 2/18/1931
The Bluest Eye

Anger is loaded with information and energy.
Audre Lorde, born 2/18/1934

*I can be an ogre at time—I guess we all can—and I
can be short. When I've gotten up on the wrong side of
the bed and I go into the office, everybody knows it. I'm
a perfectionist and I like to get everything done today.*
Jack Nicklaus, born 1/21/1940

*Yeah, I had a rage problem. I didn't know how
to deal with the situation on Moonlighting.
I threw a chair at the wall. I was accused
of throwing it at Glenn Gordon Caron.*
Cybill Shepherd, born 2/18/1950

*I had to work to reclaim my anger. It was like a hot-
water heater. I went too far. I went from not having
a voice at all to being really confrontational.*
Mary Steenburgen, born 2/8/1953

*At the same time he wanted to bolt across the
table and punch Wright's face with as much
violence as he could generate, then knock him to
the floor and kick him until he didn't move.*
John Grisham, born 2/8/1955
The Associate

*I admit it. I am not the most even-
tempered guy in the world.*
Greg Norman, born 2/10/1955

My basic problem was that I would get all tripped out by the negatives—bad calls, bad days, bad feelings—and anger got to be a habit. I was like a compulsive gambler or an alcoholic. Anger became a powerful habit.

John McEnroe, born 2/16/1959

I'm a pretty passionate person, and would need to learn to keep my emotions in check, to work with patience and a positive attitude.

Matt Dillon, born 2/18/1964

It was great having red hair as a kid because I had something to blame my temper on. Now I go for the same color palette as Conan O'Brien. I did dye it blonde once, but it backfired, as I had nothing to blame my temper on!

Isla Fisher, born 2/3/1976

I just broke my racquet; that's it. It's not so dangerous. I didn't kill anybody.

Marat Safin, born 1/27/1980

"Golf" is the only four-letter word I don't say when I'm playing it.

Justin Timberlake, born 1/31/1981

Aquarius Specialty: Temperamental Outbursts

- Marat Safin (1/27/1980) broke all his racquets during a single practice and had to have playing racquets flown in
- Christian Bale (1/30/1974) ranted and cussed for more than three minutes when a scene was interrupted by a crew member
- Gary Coleman (2/8/1968) was arrested for allegedly punching a fan

- Actress Brett Butler (1/30/1958) exhibited a wild temper on the *Grace Under Fire* set
- Virginia Woolf (1/25/1882) and Jackson Pollock (1/28/1912) went through uncontrollable rages
- Writer W. Somerset Maugham (1/25/1874) erupted into screaming frenzies
- Wolfgang Amadeus Mozart (1/27/1756) was considered temperamental
- Other Aquarians known for their rages:
  - John L. Lewis (2/12/1880)
  - Anna Pavlova (2/12/1881)
  - Tallulah Bankhead (1/31/1902)
  - Bobby Brown (2/5/1969)

Extreme Behavior

Uranus, the ruling planet of Aquarius, appears to jump in and out of its orbit, usually closer to the Sun than adjacent planet Neptune but sometimes farther away. Uranus travels above then below the plane adhered to by the other planets in their rotation around the Sun. Aquarians like shocking people. Unpredictability contributes to your unique charm, but your extreme actions can turn into monumental blunders that derail your life plans.

> *'Tis strange—but true; for truth is always strange;*
> *Stranger than fiction.*
>
> Lord Byron, born 1/22/1788
> Don Juan

*And as he spoke, he boldly took her hand and
carried it to his lips. She was astonished by the
gesture and, as she thought about it, shocked.*
Stendhal, born 1/23/1783
The Red and the Black

"Curiouser and curiouser!" cried Alice.
Lewis Carroll, born 1/27/1832
Alice in Wonderland

*But the beginning of things, of a world
especially, is necessarily vague, tangled,
chaotic, and exceedingly disturbing.*
Kate Chopin, born 2/8/1850
The Awakening

Impropriety is the soul of wit.
W. Somerset Maugham, born 1/25/1874
The Moon and Sixpence

*The beauty of the world has two edges, one of
laughter, one of anguish, cutting the heart asunder.*
Virginia Woolf, born 1/25/1882

*Irresponsibility is part of the pleasure of all art;
it is the part the schools cannot recognize.*
James Joyce, born 2/2/1882

*One time, driving Anne in my Franklin, I had to
drive through a lot, onto a lawn, and down a
six-foot hill onto another street. An old couple
rocking on a porch nearby stared silently.*
Charles Lindbergh, born 2/4/1902

If I've shocked you, darlings, I'm glad.
                    Zsa Zsa Gabor, born 2/6/1917

*One of my vanities may be that I've always
wanted my books to be provocations.*
                    Norman Mailer, born 1/31/1923

Oh, well, half of one, six dozen of the other.
                    Sportscaster Joe Garagiola, born 2/12/1926

*Happiness is excitement that has found a
settling down place, but there is always a
little corner that keeps flapping around.*
                    E.L. Konigsburg, born 2/10/1930
From the Mixed-Up Files of Mrs. Basil E. Frankweiler

*I drove away. It was a rare opportunity to do something
stupid. I'd been traumatized. I had to leave. Arthur and
the rest of the firm would just have to give me a break.*
                    John Grisham, born 2/8/1955
                    Street Lawyer

Going Rogue
Autobiographical title from Sarah Palin, born 2/11/1964

*It was sort of one of those things
that was like a perfect storm.*
                    Mischa Barton, born 1/24/1986,
about her involuntary psychiatric hospitalization

Aquarius Specialty: Off-the-Wall Action

What were you thinking?

- Marat Safin (1/27/1980) dropped his shorts after a successful drop shot in a major tournament
- After scoring a touchdown, Randy Moss (2/13/1977) pantomimed dropping his drawers and mooning opposing fans
- Baseball player Roberto Alomar (2/5/1968) spit in an umpire's face
- Nathan Lane (2/3/1956) blurted out *The Sixth Sense* movie secret on a late-night talk show
- Farrah Fawcett (2/2/1947) appeared dazed and incoherent on a late-night TV talk show
- Feminist Germaine Greer (1/29/1939) raised eyebrows with publication of a book about the sensual attraction of young boys
- Actor Gene Hackman (1/30/1931)was busted from corporal to private while serving in the military

I don't want to spend my whole life being predictable.
Farrah Fawcett, born 2/2/1947,
after her spaced-out appearance on a late-night talk show

The Green Bay thing was fun, like being
caught up in the moment. When happiness
and joy hit you, it's hard to hold it in.
Randy Moss, born 2/13/1977,
about gesturing as if dropping his drawers

Boredom

Aquarius hates being bored or boring. You pursue activity to stimulate yourself and break out of circular thinking. Aquarius should guard against the temptation to stir the pot just so you have something interesting to do.

Society is now one polished horde,
Formed of two mighty tribes,
The Bores and the Bored.

Lord Byron, born 1/22/1788
Don Juan

She wanted something to happen—something,
anything; she did not know what.

Kate Chopin, born 2/8/1850
The Awakening

However well organized the foundations of life
may be, life must always be full of risks.

Havelock Ellis, born 2/2/1859

I have been devoured all my life by an incurable
and burning impatience: and to this day
find all oratory, biography, operas, films,
plays, books, and persons, too long.

Margot Asquith, born 2/2/1864

I have not been afraid of excess: excess on occasion
is exhilarating. It prevents moderation from
acquiring the deadening effect of a habit.

W. Somerset Maugham, born 1/25/1874

*Now more than ever do I realize that I shall never be
content with a sedentary life, and that I shall always
be haunted by thoughts of a sun-drench elsewhere.*
Isabelle Eberhardt, born 2/17/1877
The Passionate Nomad

*The human soul has need of security and also
of risk. The fear of violence or of hunger or
of any other extreme evil is a sickness of the
soul. The boredom produced by a complete
absence of risk is also a sickness of the soul.*
Simone Weil, born 2/3/1909

*Every time I've touched bottom as far as boredom
is concerned, new vistas of ennui open up.*
Margaret Halsey, born 2/13/1910
No Laughing Matter

*Security is when everything is settled, when nothing
can happen to you; security is the denial of life.*
Germaine Greer, born 1/29/1939
The Female Eunuch

*I'll always push the envelope. To me, the ultimate
sin in life is to be boring. I don't play it safe.*
Cybill Shepherd, born 2/18/1950

*They came to me, and it was a total surprise. I like
to try new things because I get bored so easily. And
I like the show, so I thought it was a great idea.*
Ellen DeGeneres, born 1/28/1958

*. . . the boredom I fear away from baseball, away
from basketball, going through just a normal life . . .*
Michael Jordan, born 2/17/1963

The worst thing in the world to be is
a boring example to a child.

Christian Bale, born 1/30/1974

I get bored very easily. You move on, you do new things.

Ashton Kutcher, born 2/7/1978

Bluntness

No zodiac sign surpasses Sagittarius for foot-in-mouth disease, but Aquarius comes close. Sagittarian candor comes from a core honesty coupled with puppy-like enthusiasm for the moment at hand. Aquarian bluntness stems from your stubborn adherence to principle. Bill Russell (2/12/1934) lost the support of local basketball fans with his comments on racism in Boston. Going over the head of then-President Truman, General Douglas MacArthur (1/26/1880) presented his ideas directly to Congress; Truman promptly relieved MacArthur of his command. Political handlers quickly set safeguards against the unfiltered outspokenness of Presidential running mates Dan Quayle (2/4/1947) and Sarah Palin (2/11/1964).

Oblivion has been noticed as the offspring of silence.

Hannah More, born 2/2/1745

If you want to be witty, work on your character
and say what you think on every occasion.

Stendhal, born 1/23/1783

What is most important to me must be spoken, made verbal and shared, even at the risk of having it bruised and misunderstood. The speaking profits me, beyond any other effect.

Audre Lorde, born 2/18/1934

I refuse to sit down and shut up as they wanted.

Sarah Palin, born 2/11/1964

At Home

- Ancestor Reverence
- Child Prodigy
- Objective Parent

- Playful Grandparent
- Big Spender

Ancestor Reverence

In another Uranian turnabout, future-focused Aquarians show special reverence for distant ancestors. You often sense your ancestry generically, without reference to a specific parent or grandparent. You hold your ancestors in sacred light.

> *It takes time for the absent to assume their true shape in our thoughts. After death they take on a firmer outline and then cease to change.*
> Colette, born 1/28/1873
> Sido

For we think back through our
mothers if we are women.

Virginia Woolf, born 1/25/1882

Riverrun, past Eve and Adam's . . .

James Joyce, born 2/2/1882
Finnegans Wake

I've known rivers:
I've known rivers ancient as the world and older than the flow
of human blood in human veins.
My soul has grown deep like the rivers.

Langston Hughes, born 2/1/1902
The Negro Speaks of Rivers

When you kill the ancestor you kill yourself.

Toni Morrison, born 2/18/1931

My great-great-great-grandmother walked as a
slave from Virginia to Eatonton, Georgia . . . It
is in memory of this walk that I chose to keep
and to embrace my "maiden" name, Walker.

Alice Walker, born 2/9/1944

Child Prodigy

Aquarian genius shows at an early age. Wolfgang Amadeus Mozart (1/27/1756) composed regularly by age five, and started performing for European royalty at age six. Virtuoso violinist Jascha Heifetz (2/2/1901) first astonished audiences at age seven.

I never hear in my imagination the parts
successively. I hear them all at once. What a
delight this is! All this inventing, this producing,
takes place in a pleasing, lively dream.

Wolfgang Amadeus Mozart, born 1/27/1756

*Language was not powerful enough to
describe the infant phenomenon.*
Charles Dickens, born 2/7/1812
Nicholas Nickleby

*It is not a bad thing that children should occasionally,
and politely, put parents in their place.*
Colette, born 1/28/1873
My Mother's House

*When I was a kid, if I sang a little around the house, my parents
said, "Oh, that's good, Gregory. You should sing more. Sing,
Gregory!" If I was funny, they'd say, "Oh, that's very funny."
Anything I did, my parents encouraged me. It's made me more
positive today.*
Gregory Hines, born 2/14/1946

*When I was a little boy I used to amaze
my parents' friends by multiplying and
dividing large numbers in my head.*
John McEnroe, born 2/16/1959

*I have to admit, my childhood was a little different from most. I
could skate at two. I was nationally known at six. I was signing
autographs at ten. I had a national magazine article written
about me at eleven and a thirty-minute national television show
done on me at fifteen.*
Wayne Gretzky, born 1/26/1961

*He had such intelligence about him at such
a young age. People were fascinated.*
Shavar Ross about costar Gary Coleman, born 2/8/1968

The first, first, first, first song I wrote I was 11,
but the first good song I wrote I was 14.
Alicia Keys, born 1/25/1981

I picked one [guitar] up when I was six. Something
was really familiar about it. I just got it.
Orianthi, born 1/22/1985

Objective Parent

Capricorn talks sternly about parenthood while Sagittarius speaks with humility. Aquarius comments objectively. The Aquarian parent promptly accepts the child as its own person. Your Aquarian detachment lets your children learn lessons on their own.

Her child was like a load that held her down, and
yet like a hand that pulled her to her feet.
Edith Wharton, born 1/24/1862
Summer

Parents learn a lot from their children
about coping with life.
Muriel Spark, born 2/1/1918

Don't bail out your kid. If you have a teen who
gets in trouble with the law, let him suffer the
consequences. If the kid resents you, who cares?
Tom Selleck, born 1/29/1945

I'm very observant of what they love to do.
Michael Jordan, born 2/17/1963,
about what he does with his kids

*Everyone with adult children knows exactly
how I feel. You have to give these young
adults their wings, room to make their own
decisions and to learn from their mistakes.*
Sarah Palin, born 2/11/1964,
about her daughter Bristol

*I love that there are two people in the world that think
I'm smart, that have no agendas. It's like starting your
life all over when you have kids. It's being born again.*
Chris Rock, born 2/7/1965

*My daughters . . . saved me from my
miserable self. When I'm with my kids
and my family, it's all about them.*
Chris Rock, born 2/7/1965

*We want them to be as independent as possible. My
parents, being tall, brought me up to just get on with
it. It sounds harsh, but it's the right way to be.*
Warwick Davis, born 2/3/1970,
about his children

*I was so excited to finally meet her
and see her beautiful face.*
Denise Richards, born 2/17/1972

Playful Grandparent

Aquarius combines a silly streak with the capacity to bridge generations. Aquarians make ideal grandparents.

*I love these little people; and it is not a slight thing,
when they, who are so fresh from God, love us.*
Charles Dickens, born 2/7/1812

I tend to schedule myself around their schedules.
Sometimes I have to remember to act like
an adult, not just wait for a play date.

Alan Alda, born 1/28/1936,
about his grandkids

You don't have to worry about teaching them all the
things that one must teach their children—about
manners, what's right and what's wrong. Apple
and I just get to do really silly stuff together.

Blythe Danner, born 2/3/1943

An African belief is that the real bond is not
between you and your parents; it's between you
and your grandparents. Grandchildren help you
grow. That's part of their job in the world.

Alice Walker, born 2/9/1944

It's funny what happens when you become a
grandparent. You start to act all goofy and do
things you never thought you'd do. It's terrific.

Mike Krzyzewski, born 2/13/1947

Big Spender

Aquarians can spend money. You spend for worthwhile things
but you easily find yourself overextended. Plan, Water-Bearer, make
a plan.

Riches are for spending.

Francis Bacon, born 1/22/1561

*A little wanton money, which burned
out the bottom of his purse.*
                                    Thomas More, born 2/7/1478

Money is Aladdin's lamp.
                                    Lord Byron, born 1/22/1788

*Annual income twenty pounds, annual expenditures
nineteen pounds and six, result happiness. Annual
income twenty pounds, annual expenditure
twenty pounds and six, result misery.*
                                    Charles Dickens, born 2/7/1812

*Perhaps the most important use of money—it saves time. Life
is so short, and there's so much to do, one can't afford to waste
a minute; and just think how much you waste, for instance, in
walking from place to place instead of going by bus and in going
by bus instead of by taxi.*
                                    W. Somerset Maugham, born 1/25/1874

*Why is there so much month left
at the end of the money?*
                                    John Barrymore, born 2/15/1882

*I didn't know much about budgeting. I kept
asking the Braves for advances on my salary,
and they kept sending me money.*
                                    Hank Aaron, born 2/5/1934

I took some bad hits in a couple of business projects, a couple of developments in New York and California where I shouldn't have signed my name to the paper. They both cost me a lot of money and there was potential for my owing even more. I was in trouble. I could have owed a lot more than I was worth.

Jack Nicklaus, born 1/21/1940

Relationships

- **The Go-Between**
- **Interested Friend**
- **Aloof Date**

- **Experimental Lover**
- **Noncommittal Partner**
- **Abrupt Starts and Stops**

The Go-Between

Aquarians bridge between groups, moving without judgment between types and generations. You easily connect race with race, faction with faction, old with young. *Alice in Wonderland* by Lewis Carroll (1/27/1832) grew out of the writer's long friendship with neighboring children. Natalie Cole (2/6/1950) earned the top Grammy award for the *Unforgettable* duet with her father, a recording produced 25 years after his death.

> *Give a little love to a child, and*
> *you get a great deal back.*
> John Ruskin, born 2/8/1819

*Today we'd be Kutcher and Demi Moore. I did love her
so. But with my career and hers . . . it was difficult.*
Robert Wagner, born 2/10/1930,
about lover Barbara Stanwyck, 23 years his senior

*The sharing of joy, whether physical, emotional, psychic or
intellectual, forms a bridge between the sharers which can be
the basis for understanding much of what is not shared between
them, and lessen the threat of their difference.*
Audre Lorde, born 2/18/1934

*You grow up. But I'm probably still
younger than my kids.*
Alice Cooper, born 2/4/1948

*We measure success and depth by length and
time, but it is possible to have a deep relationship
that doesn't always stay the same.*
Barbara Hershey, born 2/5/1948

*I never went to college. But I would
totally go later in life. Go, Granny!*
Tiffani Thiessen, born 1/23/1974

*I am able to hang with the hardest, the baddest,
the worst, and I'm able to hang with the most
proper, and be at ease. I'm able to hang with any
skin color, any belief. I just fit in everywhere.*
Alicia Keys, born 1/25/1981

Aquarius Specialty: May-to-December Affairs

Many high-profile Aquarians have chosen romantic partners from outside the expected age bracket:

Aquarian	Birthdate	Partner	Sign	Years Apart
Mena Suvari	2/13/1979	Robert Brinkmann	Scorpio	17
Ashton Kutcher	2/7/1978	Demi Moore	Scorpio	16
Princess Caroline	1/23/1957	Philippe Junot	Aries	17
John Travolta	2/18/1954	Diana Hyland	Aquarius	18
Barbara Hershey	2/5/1948	Naveen Andrews	Capricorn	21
Mia Farrow	2/9/1945	Frank Sinatra	Sagittarius	29
Burt Reynolds	2/11/1936	Dinah Shore	Pisces	20
Gene Hackman	1/30/1931	Betsy Arakawa	Unknown	30
Robert Wagner	2/10/1930	Barbara Stanwyck	Cancer	23
Clark Gable	2/1/1901	Josephine Dillon	Aquarius	17
Humphrey Bogart	1/23/1899	Lauren Bacall	Virgo	25
Jimmy Durante	2/10/1893	Margie Little	Libra	28

Interested Friend

Friends are the family we choose.
Jennifer Aniston, born 2/11/1969

Aquarian curiosity and tolerance lead to an interesting assortment of friends. You thoroughly enjoy probing different points of view. Many Aquarians rely on the support system of friends rather on family and mate.

There is nothing on this earth more to
be prized than true friendship.
Thomas Aquinas, born 1/28/1225

The worst solitude is to be destitute
of sincere friendship.

Francis Bacon, born 1/22/1561

True friendship is never serene.

Madame de Sévigné, born 2/5/1626

Should auld acquaintance be forgot,
And never brought to mind?

Robert Burns, born 1/25/1759
Auld Lang Syne

I love to lose myself in other men's minds.

Charles Lamb, born 2/10/1775

The real marriage of true minds is for any two
people to possess a sense of humor or irony pitched
in exactly the same key, so that their joint glances
at any subject cross like interarching searchlights.

Edith Wharton, born 1/24/1862

She is a friend of mind. She gather me, man. The
pieces I am, she gather them and give them back to
me in all the right order. It's good, you know, when
you got a woman who is a friend of your mind.

Toni Morrison, born 2/18/1931
Beloved

Girlfriends are the best thing that
ever happened to this planet.

Natalie Cole, born 2/6/1950

Probably the telephone. I know people who are really good at having a five-minute conversation, but I can't do that. If it's a friend, I want to talk an hour. I spend a lot of time on the phone when I could be getting a degree or learning another language.

Laura Dern, born 2/1/1967,
on her worst habit

I feel beautiful when I'm laughing and surrounded by friends that know me and love me and vice versa. A good body scrub and massage do the trick as well!

Jennifer Aniston, born 2/11/1969

I have three best friends—Alison, Michael, and Nadia—whom I've known a minimum of 15 years each . . . You can't describe the chemistry that keeps friends together other than they've managed to stick with you.

Heather Graham, born 1/29/1970

Aloof Date

All astrological signs have ways to attract others. Sagittarian sexuality carouses, Virgo tries to cover up, while Scorpio oozes sexual mystery. Cool, breezy Aquarius plays from a distance. Aquarian detachment makes intimacy difficult. Turning love into a concept helps you keep others at arm's length.

They do best who, if they cannot but admit love, yet make it keep quarter; and sever it wholly from their serious affairs and actions of life.

Francis Bacon, born 1/22/1561

He's aloof, unfortunate creature that I am! To see the most indecent advances repulsed! And repulsed by one of my father's servants.

Stendhal, born 1/23/1783

Snails were capable of affection up to a certain point.
Charles Darwin, born 2/12/1809

"Bah," said Scrooge. "Humbug!"
Charles Dickens, born 2/7/1812
A Christmas Carol

*No one can do me any good by loving me; I have more
love than I need, or could do any good with; but people
do me good by making me love them—which isn't easy.*
John Ruskin, born 2/8/1819

Intimacy is a difficult art.
Virginia Woolf, born 1/25/1882

*Do not allow yourself to be imprisoned by any affection. Keep
your solitude. The day, if it ever comes, when you are given true
affection there will be no opposition between interior solitude
and friendship, quite the reverse. It is even by this infallible sign
that you will recognize it.*
Simone Weil, born 2/3/1909

*Loneliness is never more cruel than when
it is felt in close propinquity with someone
who has ceased to communicate.*
Germaine Greer, born 1/29/1939

*All who would win joy must share it;
happiness was born a twin.*
Lord Byron, born 1/22/1788

*The question of love is one that cannot be evaded. Whether or
not you claim to be interested in it, from the moment you are
alive you are bound to be concerned with love, because love is*

not just something that happens to you: It is a certain special way of being alive. Love is, in fact, an intensification of life, a completeness, a fullness, a wholeness of life.

Thomas Merton, born 1/31/1915

Experimental Lover

*I don't seem to find much of a difference
between women and men when it comes to
loving them. If they're wonderful, sexy, and cute,
I want to snuggle up and be enchanted.*

Alice Walker, born 2/9/1944
Now Is the Time to Open Your Heart

Some Aquarians engage in nontraditional affairs. All signs encompass all sexual preferences but, with greater incidence than other signs, Aquarius provides historical examples of sexual experimentation. Astrological writers link Aquarius with the myth of Ganymede, the beautiful boy stolen by Jupiter to become the cupbearer of the Olympian gods.

O fie, miss, you must not kiss and tell.

William Congreve, born 1/24/1670
Love for Love

. . . felt herself struck by Julien's unusual beauty. His almost feminine features, and his embarrassment, did not seem in any way ridiculous to a woman herself so extraordinarily shy. The masculine ways people thought necessary, for a man to be handsome, made her afraid.

Stendhal, born 1/23/1783
The Red and the Black

No woman has ever slept with me too soon.
I don't pretend I'm typical, but I've always
found promiscuous women interesting.

Norman Mailer, born 1/31/1923

Well, I'm certainly not going through life
with one hand tied behind my back.

James Dean, born 2/8/1931,
who refused to answer questions about his sexual orientation

We tend to think of the erotic as an easy,
tantalizing sexual arousal. I speak of the erotic
as the deepest life force, a force which moves
us toward living in a fundamental way.

Audre Lorde, born 2/18/1934

Aquarius Specialty: Sexual Experiments

- Tallulah Bankhead (1/31/1902) and James Dean (2/8/1931) dallied with both men and women
- Virginia Woolf (1/25/1882) had an intense love affair with poet Vita Sackville-West
- W. Somerset Maugham (1/25/1874) was bisexual
- Poets Amy Lowell (2/9/1874) and Gertrude Stein (2/3/1874) were open lesbians
- Colette (1/28/1873) experimented with transvestites and with younger men
- Lord Byron (1/22/1788) earned a reputation as a great lover

Noncommittal Partner

Aquarius is so intent on expressing individuality that you resist commitment to a relationship. You hesitate to become permanently identified with someone else. Once you're formally attached, Aquarian loyalty matches that of most other zodiac signs.

> *From my experience of life I believe my personal*
> *motto should be "Beware of men bearing flowers."*
> Muriel Spark, born 2/1/1918
> Curriculum Vitae

> *I haven't met someone else. And if I did, then I'd*
> *have to worry about their food, their shirts, their*
> *work. I'm not sure I want to do that again.*
> Mia Farrow, born 2/9/1945

> *I am finally the woman my mother always wanted me to be. I find myself pleased with myself and with my solitude. I would love to have a life partner who was a great conversationalist and is funny, and thought I was funny. Honesty and a sense of confidence are important. Not the money so much.*
> Cybill Shepherd, born 2/18/1950

> *To be really honest, I'd have to say I'm afraid of committing to one person, so I have maybe three or four people on the line . . . But I feel I have to come clean about my situation because it can come apart at any minute, and I don't like that feeling. I like everyone I'm involved with, and I never want to lose those friendships. Romance has a tendency to confuse friendships, and I don't want that.*
> John Travolta, born 2/18/1954,
> before settling down with Kelly Preston

[Her parents' divorce] made me one of those people who
say, "I'm going to be completely self-dependent, because
I don't want a relationship to be based on finances."
Jennifer Aniston, born 2/11/1969

There's something very claustrophobic
about the idea of marriage for me.
Shakira, born 2/2/1977

Don't ever be the one to say, "What are we?"
Lauren Conrad, born 2/1/1986,
her #1 dating no-no

Abrupt Starts and Stops

Of all the gin joints in all the towns in
all the world, she walks into mine.
Humphrey Bogart, born 1/23/1899
Casablanca

Frankly, my dear, I don't give a damn.
Clark Gable, born 2/1/1901
Gone With the Wind

The Aquarian pattern of sudden transition extends into relationships. Even in the movies, Aquarius provides the most memorable instances of sudden attraction and abrupt departure. Aquarius takes but an instant to plug into a new romance, and your breakups can be equally abrupt.

A wise woman never yields by appointment.
Stendhal, born 1/23/1783

I shall not say why and how I became, at the age
of fifteen, the mistress of the Earl of Craven.
Harriette Wilson, 2/2/1786

*When a man and a woman see each other and like
each other they ought to come together—wham—
like a couple of taxis on Broadway, not sit around
analyzing each other like two specimens in a bottle.*
Thelma Ritter, born 2/14/1902
Rear Window

*He always came to her unexpectedly—and she liked it, because
it made him a continuous presence in her life, like the ray of a
hidden light that could hit her at any moment.*
Ayn Rand, born 2/2/1905
Atlas Shrugged

*I love the company of women. I fall in love superfast, and I'll
want to spend the next week together, 24 hours a day. I will
drop everything when it's starting, and that's stupid. If you're
not going to take a week off on a regular basis, then don't do it
in the beginning.*
Ashton Kutcher, born 2/7/1978

A lucky marriage pays for all.
Madame de Sévigné, born 2/5/1626

*Accident counts for much in
companionship as in marriage.*
Henry Adams, born 2/16/1838
The Education of Henry Adams

*Heaven has no rage like love to hatred turned
nor hell a fury like a woman scorned.*
William Congreve, born 1/24/1670

Friendship is a vase, which, when it is flawed by heat or violence or accident, may as well be broken at once; it can never be trusted after. The more graceful and ornamental it was, the more clearly do we discern the hopelessness of restoring it to its former state. Coarse stones, if they are fractured, may be cemented again; precious ones never.

Walter Savage Landor, born 1/30/1775

I have lost friends, some by death . . . others through sheer inability to cross the street.

Virginia Woolf, born 1/25/1882
The Waves

"Get out," I said, crying hard. "What am I supposed to tell the kids? That their father wants to marry their sister?"

Mia Farrow, born 2/9/1945

When something bad happens to me, I think I'm able to deal with it in a pretty good way. That makes me lucky. Some people fall apart at the first little thing that happens.

Christie Brinkley, born 2/2/1954,
after her then-husband's cheating scandal

When the car was full, I left a note telling her I was gone. I placed it next to the one she'd left, and refused to stare at it. My emotions were mixed and just under the skin, and I was not equipped to deal with them. I'd never moved out before; I wasn't sure how it was done.

John Grisham, born 2/8/1955
Street Lawyer

It's sad when someone you know
becomes someone you knew.
Henry Rollins, born 2/13/1961

I left our home to work on a movie, and while I
was away, my boyfriend got married, and I've never
heard from him again . . . it's like a sudden death.
Laura Dern, born 2/1/1967,
about Billy Bob Thornton with Angelina Jolie

The relationship [Lance Armstrong] had been falling
apart over time anyway. But becoming a public tidbit
of news interest and then . . . It's a real showstopper
when you get diagnosed with breast cancer.
Sheryl Crow, born 2/11/1962

Sit in it, be with it, be in it. There is such a
freedom, in a weird way, to say, "Look, here I
am, this is it." You move through it faster.
Jennifer Aniston, born 2/11/1969,
about her survival mantra after Pitt breakup

Everything exploded that night . . . With my heart pounding, I
left. I'll never forget my scramble through the house. Shaking
and terrified, I packed a suitcase, put my daughter in the car,
and explained to our confused housekeeper why I wanted her to
come.
Denise Richards, born 2/17/1972,
about leaving Charlie Sheen

Aquarius Specialty: Sudden Breakups

More than any other sign, Aquarians earn headlines for sudden romantic endings.

- The high-profile marriage of Kim Kardashian and Aquarian Kris Humphries (2/6/1985) lasted 72 days
- Demi Moore quickly divorced Aquarian Ashton Kutcher (2/7/1978) when stories of his infidelities surfaced
- Aquarian Jennifer Aniston (2/11/1969) was left behind when husband Brad Pitt connected with Angelina Jolie
- Aquarian Lisa Marie Presley (2/1/1968) married Michael Jackson 20 days after divorcing her husband of six years. Presley and Jackson divorced less than two years later.
- Billy Bob Thornton jilted Aquarian Laura Dern (2/1/1967) when he abruptly married Angelina Jolie in 2000
- Aquarian Greg Norman (2/10/1955) and Chris Evert divorced after 18 months of marriage
- Aquarian Carol Channing (1/31/1923) abruptly left her husband after 41 years of marriage

Famous Aquarius Relationships

Romantic compatibility is the most popular area of astrological inquiry and one of the most complex. The Sun-sign relationship describing the core energy flow between two individuals is based on each sign's traits and on relative location within the zodiac circle. Here are astrology's traditional assessments of the Aquarian's compatibility with other zodiac signs:

Aquarian's Partner	Usual Dates	Energy Flow	Relation to Aquarius on the Zodiac Circle
Taurus	Apr. 20 through May 20	Challenging	Square (90 degrees)
Scorpio	Oct. 23 through Nov. 22	Challenging	Square (90 degrees)

Aquarius	Jan. 20 through Feb. 18	Neutral	None (0 degrees)
Cancer	Jun. 21 through Jul. 21	Neutral	Weak (150 degrees)
Virgo	Aug. 23 through Sept. 21	Neutral	Weak (150 degrees)
Pisces	Feb. 19 through Mar. 20	Positive	Adjacent (30 degrees)
Capricorn	Dec. 22 through Jan. 19	Positive	Adjacent (30 degrees)
Aries	Mar. 21 through Apr. 19	Positive	Sextile (60 degrees)
Sagittarius	Nov. 23 through Dec. 21	Positive	Sextile (60 degrees)
Gemini	May 21 through Jun. 20	Very Positive	Triangle (120 degrees)
Libra	Sept. 22 through Oct. 22	Very Positive	Triangle (120 degrees)
Leo	Jul. 22 through Aug. 22	Very Positive	Opposite (180 degrees)

Certain Sun placements are more likely to generate mutually beneficial relationships with Aquarians. But the following tables prove that Aquarius forms both successful and unsuccessful relationships with individuals from each zodiac sign. Sun signs tell only part of the story indicated by a full comparison of individual birth charts. The zodiac sign of each individual's Moon and the interaction of the planets also impact the relationship. One person's astrological talents and challenges can complement, antagonize or have little impact on another person's natural tendencies. Visit a qualified astrologer for additional insight into your relationship potential. For a list of recommended astrologers, go to www.quotablezodiac.com.

Astrology indicates tendencies, but individuals still exercise free will within relationships. There are no quick answers to getting along well with someone else. Astrological awareness can help two individuals blend their natural characteristics to mutual advantage.

Challenging: Aquarius with Taurus

Tradition divides zodiac signs into three types of action—Cardinal (dynamic), Fixed (purposeful) and Mutable (adaptable). Fixed signs Scorpio, Leo, Taurus and Aquarius are characterized by the unwavering determination to get what you want. But Taurus

conserves while Aquarius innovates. Sturdy Taurus plods steadily along while Aquarius leapfrogs to whole new levels. Two stubborn individuals moving at different speeds can limit progress within the relationship itself.

Aquarian	Birthdate	Taurus	Relationship
Lauren Conrad	2/1/1986	Audrina Patridge	Feuding costar
Eddie Van Halen	1/26/1957	Valerie Bertinelli	Spouse, divorced
Christie Brinkley	2/2/1954	Billy Joel	Spouse, divorced
Alice Cooper	2/4/1948	Glen Campbell	Golfing friend
Mikhail Baryshnikov	1/27/1948	Jessica Lange	Lover, parent
Farrah Fawcett	2/2/1947	Alana Stewart	Best friend
Farrah Fawcett	2/2/1947	Ryan O'Neal	Domestic partner, split; friend
Farrah Fawcett	2/2/1947	Lee Majors	Spouse, divorced
Sonny Bono	2/16/1935	Cher	Musical partner; spouse, divorced
Bess Truman	2/13/1885	Harry Truman	Spouse
Douglas MacArthur	1/26/1880	Harry Truman	Boss who fired him
Gertrude Stein	2/3/1874	Alice B. Toklas	Longtime partner
Julia Grant	1/26/1826	Ulysses S. Grant	Spouse

Adventure is the life of commerce, but caution, I had almost said timidity, is the life of banking.
Walter Bagehot, born 2/3/1826
Lombard Street

His car was red because he loved red. He was a Taurus, and every other Taurus he knew also loved red and owned a red car.
Alice Walker, born 2/9/1944
Now Is the Time to Open Your Heart

Challenging: Aquarius with Scorpio

Aquarius Sun-sign individuals are challenged by the square relationship with Scorpio. The Aquarian's cool intellectualism

doesn't mix with Scorpio's emotional intensity. The Aquarian's involvement in social issues challenges Scorpio's self-protective isolation. The Aquarian's egalitarian perspective doesn't accommodate Scorpio's subtle maneuvers for power. But the following supposedly difficult relationships include some well-known, long-lasting relationships. To all appearances, Aquarians Danny Moder and Camila Alves enjoy committed relationships with Scorpios. Neither association seems to suffer from the A-list celebrity status of the Scorpio partner. As within an individual's birth-chart, great strength comes from overcoming the tension of the square.

Aquarius	Birthdate	Scorpio	Relationship
Camila Alves	1/28/1982	Matt McConaughey	Fiancé
Ashton Kutcher	2/7/1978	Demi Moore	Spouse, dvorced
Jerry O'Connell	2/17/1974	Rebecca Romijn	Spouse
Jennifer Aniston	2/11/1969	David Schwimmer	Off-and-on TV pair
Danny Moder	1/31/1969	Julia Roberts	Spouse
Laura Dern	2/1/1967	Ben Harper	Spouse, divorced
Diane Lane	1/22/1965	Elizabeth Perkins	Best friend
John McEnroe	2/16/1959	Tatum O'Neal	Spouse, divorced
Vanna White	2/18/1957	Pat Sajak	Wheel of Fortune cohost
Christopher Guest	2/5/1948	Jamie Lee Curtis	Spouse
Tom Smothers	2/2/1937	Dick Smothers	Brother, comedy partner
Burt Reynolds	2/11/1936	Sally Field	Lover, split
Robert Wagner	2/10/1930	Stefanie Powers	Hart to Hart costar
Jackson Pollock	1/28/1912	Lee Krasner	Spouse
Clark Gable	2/1/1901	Vivien Leigh	Gone with the Wind costar
Soong Ching-ling	1/27/1893	Sun Yat-sen	Spouse, coleader
James Joyce	2/2/1882	Ezra Pound	Literary mentor
Lord Byron	1/22/1788	Caroline Lamb	Lover

It is the wisdom of the crocodiles, that
shed tears when they would devour.
Francis Bacon, born 1/22/1561

After a while I murmured to Picasso that I like his
portrait of Gertrude Stein. Yes, he said, everybody
said that she does not look like it but that does
not make any difference, she will, he said.
Gertrude Stein, born 2/3/1874
The Autobiography of Alice B. Toklas

[Tatum] said then and later that I bullied her. But
the truth was, she always gave as good as she got.
John McEnroe about Tatum O'Neal

Neutral: Aquarius with Aquarius

Most relationships with the same Sun sign bring together too much of the same traits. The most successful same-sign partnership is Libra with Libra, where each individual's constant adjustment to the other person keeps the focus on the relationship. Aquarius with Aquarius scores as the zodiac's second most successful same-sign pairing. Aquarians form a mutual admiration society, enjoying an assortment of fascinating friends and lives full of surprises. Beware: the impractical Aquarius-Aquarius pair overspends with ease and lacks life planning skills.

Aquarius	Birthdate	Aquarius	Birthdate	Relationship
Emma Roberts	2/10/1991	Chord Overstreet	2/17/1989	Boyfriend
Paris Hilton	2/17/1981	Nick Carter	1/28/1980	Lover, split
Jennifer Aniston	2/11/1969	Kathy Najimy	2/6/1957	Longtime friend
Jennifer Aniston	2/11/1969	Sheryl Crow	2/11/1962	Longtime friend
Jennifer Aniston	2/11/1969	Laura Dern	2/1/1967	Close friend
Josh Brolin	2/12/1968	Diane Lane	1/22/1965	Spouse

Ellen DeGeneres	1/26/1958	Portia de Rossi	1/31/1973	Spouse
John Travolta	2/18/1954	Lisa Marie Presley	2/1/1968	Longtime friend
Jill Eikenberry	1/21/1947	Michael Tucker	2/6/1945	Spouse
Tallulah Bankhead	1/31/1902	Estelle Winwood	1/24/1883	Close friend

Everything about Portia impresses me. To come out of such a dark place—I can't imagine the strength that took.
Ellen DeGeneres, born 1/28/1958

We went to Turks and Caicos. It was a full five-star splurge. That was miserable . . . We said, "Let's get out of here." And went to Key West. We rented Jet Skis and took a four-hour trek around the island. She's a hoot.
Josh Brolin about Diane Lane

She celebrates her life so beautifully that I think it's the reason she's able to give so beautifully.
Jennifer Aniston, born 2/11/1969,
about Aquarian Oprah Winfrey

Neutral: Aquarius with Cancer

The Aquarius Sun is 150 degrees of the zodiac away from Cancer, making a weak connection if any. Elements other than the Sun signs generally hold these relationships together. Aquarius and Cancer live at cross purposes, with Aquarius seeking societal well-being and Cancer dedicated to home and family. Cancer nurtures; Aquarius inquires. Cancer seeks to preserve the past while Aquarius drives toward the future. The enduring marriage of Aquarian Ronald Reagan and Cancer Nancy Reagan underscores that, like all signs, Aquarius can form satisfying relationships with any sign of the zodiac.

Aquarius	Birthdate	Cancer	Relationship
Denise Richards	2/17/1972	Richie Sambora	Boyfriend, split
Rob Thomas	2/14/1972	Santana	Collaborator: Smooth
John McEnroe	2/16/1959	Patty Smyth	Spouse
John Belushi	1/24/1949	Dan Aykroyd	Blues Brother
Robert Wagner	2/10/1930	Natalie Wood	Spouse (2x)
Robert Wagner	2/10/1930	Barbara Stanwyck	Lover
Paul Newman	1/26/1925	A.E. Hotchner	Friend, business partner
Dick Martin	1/30/1922	Dan Rowan	Laugh-In cohost
Ronald Reagan	2/6/1911	Nancy Reagan	Spouse
Charles Lindbergh	2/4/1902	Anne Morrow Lindbergh	Spouse
Louisa Adams	2/12/1775	John Quincy Adams	Spouse

She was real and cute and sexy, but she
was a woman, not a girl; someone who
had lived life and knew the score.

John McEnroe about first meeting Patty Smyth

Neutral: Aquarius with Virgo

The Aquarius Sun is 150 degrees of the zodiac circle away from Virgo, making a weak connection if any. The two signs operate on different wavelengths. Virgo's social and sexual reserve doesn't mesh with Aquarian curiosity and experimentation. Virgo gladly helps specific individuals while Aquarian humanitarianism supports the cause but avoids personal contact. The following Aquarius-Virgo examples include both divorces and lasting marriages. Elements other than the Sun signs generally hold the Aquarius-Virgo combination together.

Aquarius	Birthdate	Virgo	Relationship
Paris Hilton	2/17/1981	Nicole Richie	Friend
Justin Timberlake	1/31/1981	Cameron Diaz	Lover, split
Robbie Williams	2/13/1974	Rachel Hunter	Lover, split

The Quotable Aquarius

Denise Richards	2/17/1972	Charlie Sheen	Spouse, divorced
Lisa Marie Presley	2/1/1968	Michael Jackson	Spouse, divorced
Diane Lane	1/22/1965	Richard Gere	Movie costar (3x)
Sheryl Crow	2/11/1962	Lance Armstrong	Lover, split
Garth Brooks	2/7/1962	Trisha Yearwood	Spouse
Carey Lowell	2/11/1961	Richard Gere	Spouse
Sinead Cusack	2/18/1948	Jeremy Irons	Spouse
Joy Philbin	2/1/1941	Regis Philbin	Spouse
Jack Nicklaus	1/21/1940	Arnold Palmer	Golf rival; friend
George Segal	2/13/1934	Elliott Gould	Good friend
Humphrey Bogart	1/23/1899	Ingrid Bergman	Movie costar
Humphrey Bogart	1/23/1899	Lauren Bacall	Spouse, costar

My friends say I have to get back on the bike,
and I keep saying, "Maybe not a bike."

Sheryl Crow,
after breaking up with Lance Armstrong

I'm convinced there's some past life
stuff we're working out.

Diane Lane,
about her onscreen chemistry with Richard Gere

Nicole always makes me laugh.

Paris Hilton about Nicole Richie

Positive: Aquarius with Pisces

Sensitive Pisces adds compassion to the Aquarian's abstract thinking, while purposeful Aquarius helps Pisces focus. Instinctive Pisces and intuitive Aquarius share a sixth sense about the world.

Pisces lies next to Aquarius in the zodiac circle. Adjacent astrological signs often enjoy solid relationships due to the high likelihood of overlapping zodiac signs for Mercury, planet of communication,

and Venus, planet of affection. As seen from Earth, inner planets Mercury and Venus can be located no more than 28 and 48 degrees, respectively, from the individual's Sun. For any person with Sun in Aquarius, Mercury must be in Capricorn, Aquarius or Pisces. Venus is apt to be located in Capricorn, Aquarius or Pisces. Pisces celebrities Jessica Biel and Jon Hamm were born with Venus in Aquarius, matching the Sun signs of their longtime Aquarian lovers. Shared zodiac signs bring similar characteristics that enhance compatibility.

Aquarius	Birthdate	Pisces	Relationship
Paris Hilton	2/17/1981	Benji Madden	Lover, split
Justin Timberlake	1/31/1981	Jessica Biel	Off-and-on lover
Amy Robach	2/6/1973	Andrew Shue	Spouse
Jennifer Westfeldt	2/2/1970	Jon Hamm	Longtime partner
Jennifer Aniston	2/11/1969	Chelsea Handler	Good friend
Chynna Phillips	2/12/1968	Billy Baldwin	Spouse
Bridget Fonda	1/27/1964	Peter Fonda	Father
Princess Caroline (Monaco)	1/23/1957	Ernst August	Spouse
Oprah Winfrey	1/29/1954	Stedman Graham	Longtime boyfriend
Natalie Cole	2/6/1950	Nat King Cole	Father; music collaborator
Rick James	2/1/1948	Teena Marie	Mentee; fiancée, split
Carole King	2/9/1942	James Taylor	Friend
Burt Reynolds	2/11/1936	Dinah Shore	Lover
Paul Newman	1/26/1925	Joanne Woodward	Spouse
Virginia Woolf	1/25/1882	Vita Sackville-West	Lover

I adore her. She's hot, hilarious and has a heart of gold.
Jennifer Aniston about Chelsea Handler

Positive: Aquarius with Capricorn

Capricorn organizational skills help actualize Aquarian vision and ideals. The Aquarian's sudden progress complements the Capricorn's step-by-step accomplishment. The signs share social distance—Capricorn due to shyness, Aquarius due to intellectual preoccupation.

Capricorn lies next to Aquarius in the zodiac circle. Adjacent astrological signs often enjoy solid relationships due to the high like-lihood of overlapping zodiac signs for Mercury, planet of commu-nication, and Venus, planet of affection. As seen from Earth, inner planets Mercury and Venus can be located no more than 28 and 48 degrees, respectively, from the individual's Sun. For any person with Sun in Aquarius, Mercury must be in Capricorn, Aquarius or Pisces. Venus is apt to be located in Capricorn, Aquarius or Pisces. Shared zodiac signs bring similar characteristics that enhance com-patibility. Venus in Aquarius for Capricorns Ted Danson and Christy Turlington matches the Sun in Aquarius for their spouses. Aquarian Edward Burns, Turlington's husband, further strengthens the bond with his reciprocal Venus placement in Capricorn.

Aquarius	Birthdate	Capricorn	Relationship
Tiffani Thiessen	1/23/1974	Brady Smith	Spouse
Roberto Alomar	2/5/1968	Mary Pierce	Fiancée, split
Lisa Marie Presley	2/1/1968	Nicolas Cage	Spouse, divorced
Edward Burns	1/29/1968	Christy Turlington	Spouse
George Stephanopoulos	2/10/1961	Ali Wentworth	Spouse
Wayne Gretzky	1/26/1961	Mark Messier	Hockey teammate
Wayne Gretzky	1/26/1961	Janet Jones	Spouse
Nicolas Sarkozy	1/28/1955	Carla Bruni	Spouse
Oprah Winfrey	1/29/1954	Gayle King	Close friend
Mary Steenburgen	2/8/1953	Ted Danson	Spouse

Cybill Shepherd	2/18/1950	Elvis Presley	Lover, split
Barbara Hershey	2/5/1948	Naveen Andrews	Domestic partner, split
Mike Farrell	2/6/1939	Shelley Fabares	Spouse
Ronald Reagan	2/6/1911	Jane Wyman	Spouse, divorced
Clark Gable	2/1/1901	Loretta Young	Lover, parent

He's a fascinating human being. He's as deep
as they come, as funny as they come.
Mary Steenburgen about Ted Danson

Positive: Aquarius with Aries

Aquarius Air and Aries Fire blend well together without either element overwhelming the other. Aquarius vision complements Aries action. Between Aries impetuosity and Aquarian unpredictability, the pair moves with erratic stops and starts. But it works! Aries forward impetus plus Aquarian leaps and bounds makes this the fastest-moving pair of the zodiac.

Aquarius	Birthdate	Aries	Relationship
Lauren Conrad	2/1/1986	Kyle Howard	Boyfriend, split
Jennifer Aniston	2/11/1969	Vince Vaughn	Lover, split; friend
Mariska Hargitay	1/23/1964	Christopher Meloni	Television costar
Arpad Busson	1/27/1963	Elle MacPherson	Lover, parent
Alan Bates	2/17/1934	Julie Christie	Movie costar
Bill Russell	2/12/1934	John Havlicek	Basketball teammate
Maria von Trapp	1/26/1905	Georg von Trapp	Spouse, musical partner

The sun has set in your life; it is getting cold.
The hundreds of people around you cannot
console you for the loss of the one.
Maria von Trapp after her husband's death

*Everybody seemed to think I was going to be having
fist fights with Russell. But it was the easiest damn
thing ever. He's just no-nonsense, that's all.*

Christian Bale, born 1/30/1974,
about Aries costar Russell Crowe

Positive: Aquarius with Sagittarius

Intellectual Aquarius (Air) and enthusiastic Sagittarius (Fire) combine easily without one element overwhelming the other. Sagittarius adds warmth to Aquarian objectivity while Aquarian purpose stabilizes Sagittarian scatter. Aquarian innovation stimulates Sagittarian curiosity; the Sagittarian's breadth of vision can accommodate Aquarian genius.

In the 1967 movie *Camelot*, Sagittarian Franco Nero played Lancelot to the Guinevere of Aquarian Vanessa Redgrave. The pair lived together for several years, then moved on to other relationships. Nero and Redgrave reconnected and married in 2006.

Aquarius	Birthdate	Sagittarius	Relationship
Justin Timberlake	1/31/1981	Britney Spears	Girlfriend, split
Justin Timberlake	1/31/1981	Trace Ayala	Friend, business partner
Josh Kelley	1/30/1980	Katherine Heigl	Spouse
Michael C. Hall	2/1/1971	Jennifer Carpenter	Spouse, divorced
Jennifer Aniston	2/11/1969	Brad Pitt	Spouse, divorced
Greg Norman	2/10/1955	Chris Evert	Spouse, divorced
Oprah Winfrey	1/29/1954	Tina Turner	Friend
Jane Seymour	2/15/1951	Joe Lando	Medicine Woman costar
Mia Farrow	2/9/1945	Frank Sinatra	Spouse, divorced
Mia Farrow	2/9/1945	Woody Allen	Domestic partner, split
Blythe Danner	2/3/1943	Bruce Paltrow	Spouse
Roger Staubach	2/5/1942	Bob Hayes	Football partner
Vanessa Redgrave	1/30/1937	Franco Nero	Costar; spouse

Roger Vadim	1/26/1928	Jane Fonda	Spouse, divorced
Harvey Korman	2/15/1927	Tim Conway	Comedy partner
Lana Turner	2/8/1921	Kirk Douglas	Movie costar
Ernest Borgnine	1/24/1917	Tim Conway	McHale's Navy costar
Lillian Disney	2/15/1899	Walt Disney	Spouse
Virginia Woolf	1/25/1882	Leonard Woolf	Spouse
Abraham Lincoln	2/12/1809	Mary Todd Lincoln	Spouse
Charles Lamb	2/10/1775	Mary Anne Lamb	Sister, collaborator
Francis II (France)	2/12/1768	Mary Queen of Scots	Spouse

We spent seven very intense years together . . . a
beautiful, complicated relationship . . . I really do
hope that someday we can be friends again.

Jennifer Aniston about Brad Pitt

Very Positive: Aquarius with Gemini

Aquarius and Gemini are air signs—literate, quick, glib within the world of ideas. Both exercise a wide-ranging curiosity; both have silly streaks. Aquarius moves Gemini beyond the details to the big picture; Gemini keeps Aquarius connected to the circumstances at hand. Aquarius-Gemini is the zodiac's most conversational pairing.

Aquarius	Birthdate	Gemini	Relationship
Shakira	2/2/1977	Wyclef Jean	Friend, collaborator
Big Boi	2/1/1975	Dre	OutKast partner
Jennifer Aniston	2/11/1969	Courteney Cox	BFF
Chynna Phillips	2/12/1968	Michelle Phillips	Mother
Laura Linney	2/5/1964	Jeanne Tripplehorn	Close friend
Clint Black	2/4/1962	Lisa Hartman Black	Spouse
John McEnroe	2/16/1959	Bjorn Borg	Tennis rival
Ellen DeGeneres	1/26/1958	Anne Heche	Lover, split
Ellen DeGeneres	1/26/1958	Melissa Etheridge	Friend

Mary Steenburgen	2/8/1953	Malcolm McDowell	Spouse, divorced
Donna Hanover	2/13/1950	Rudi Giuliani	Spouse, divorced
Gene Siskel	1/26/1946	Roger Ebert	Movie critic partner
William McKinley	1/29/1843	Ida McKinley	Spouse
Nell Gwyn	2/2/1650	King Charles II (Eng.)	Mistress

> *We always collaborate. You have two minds*
> *going; you put everything out on the table,*
> *sauté it and see what comes out.*
>
> Big Boi about Dre

Very Positive: Aquarius with Libra

Air signs Libra and Aquarius are thoughtful, talkative and idealistic. Libra's one-on-one attention breaks down the Aquarian's arms-length objectivity. Purposeful Aquarius helps Libra decide. Libra-Aquarius is the astrological pairing with the greatest concern for societal needs.

Aquarius	Birthdate	Libra	Relationship
Kris Humphries	2/6/1985	Kim Kardashian	Spouse, divorced
Paris Hilton	2/17/1981	Nicky Hilton	Sister
Isla Fisher	2/3/1976	Sacha Baron Cohen	Spouse
Jennifer Aniston	2/11/1969	John Mayer	Lover, split
Michael Sheen	2/2/1969	Rachel McAdams	Lover
Dr. Dre	2/18/1965	Snoop Dogg	Music partner
Dr. Dre	2/18/1965	Eminem	Music partner
Michael Jordan	2/17/1963	Scottie Pippen	Basketball teammate
Geena Davis	1/21/1956	Susan Sarandon	Friend, movie costar
John Travolta	2/18/1954	Kelly Preston	Spouse
John Travolta	2/18/1954	Olivia Newton-John	Grease costar
Blythe Danner	2/3/1943	Gwyneth Paltrow	Daughter; close
Yoko Ono	2/18/1933	John Lennon	Spouse

Roger Vadim	1/26/1928	Catherine Deneuve	Domestic partner, split
Roger Vadim	1/26/1928	Brigitte Bardot	Spouse, divorced
Jack Lemmon	2/8/1925	Felicia Farr	Spouse
Jack Lemmon	2/8/1925	Walter Matthau	Costar (9 movies), best friend
Norman Mailer	1/31/1923	Gore Vidal	Literary foe
Ronald Reagan	2/6/1911	Margaret Thatcher	Political ally
Clark Gable	2/1/1901	Carole Lombard	Spouse
Franklin Roosevelt	1/30/1882	Eleanor Roosevelt	Spouse
D.W. Griffith	1/22/1875	Lillian Gish	Friend, collaborator

Her many achievements will be
appreciated more as time goes on.
Ronald Reagan about Margaret Thatcher

She's a fabulous dancer. On occasion we have
dinner and dance between courses. We'll do
our Appetizer Dance and Soup Dance.
John Travolta about wife Kelly Preston

Very Positive: Aquarius with Leo

Opposites attract. Aquarius and Leo oppose each other on the zodiac circle and generally form complementary relationships. Both Aquarius and Leo carry high principles—Leo about the individual's obligation to do the right thing and Aquarius about society's responsibility to do the right thing. Leo gets absorbed in Self while Aquarius gets absorbed in Others. Independent Aquarius maintains identity and perspective without getting overshadowed by Leo's dramatic presence.

Aquarius	Birthdate	Leo	Relationship
Bonnie Wright	2/17/1991	Daniel Radcliffe	Harry Potter movie boyfriend
Lauren Conrad	2/1/1986	Brody Jenner	Boyfriend, split
Justin Timberlake	1/31/1981	Mila Kunis	Movie costar
Alicia Keys	1/25/1981	Swizz Beatz	Spouse
Jennifer Aniston	2/11/1969	Adam Duritz	Boyfriend, split
Bobby Brown	2/5/1969	Whitney Houston	Spouse, divorced
Michael Sheen	2/2/1969	Kate Beckinsale	Domestic partner, split
Laura Dern	2/1/1967	Billy Bob Thornton	Lover, split
Mariska Hargitay	1/23/1964	Peter Hermann	Spouse
Princess Caroline	1/23/1957	Charlotte of Monaco	Daughter
Cybill Shepherd	2/18/1950	Peter Bogdanovich	Longtime lover, split
Dick Cheney	1/30/1941	Lynne Cheney	Spouse
Burt Reynolds	2/11/1936	Loni Anderson	Spouse, divorced
Bill Russell	2/12/1934	Wilt Chamberlain	Basketball rival
Bill Russell	2/12/1934	Bob Cousy	Basketball teammate
Gene Hackman	1/30/1931	Dustin Hoffman	Friend
Robert Wagner	2/10/1930	Jill St. John	Spouse
Paul Newman	1/26/1925	Robert Redford	Movie costar
Ann Sothern	1/22/1909	Lucille Ball	Close friend
Humphrey Bogart	1/23/1899	John Huston	Close friend
W.C. Fields	1/29/1880	Mae West	Movie costar
Lord Byron	1/22/1788	Percy Bysshe Shelley	Friend
William Henry Harrison	2/9/1773	Anna Harrison	Spouse
Louis XV (France)	2/15/1710	Madame du Barry	Mistress

I bring him out, he brings me in; he slows me down, I make him go faster . . . Sometimes we want to do really different things, and that is hard to navigate. We have to sit down and figure out how to carve this time out for you and this for me, because we need both. That's just the way we are, so let's just make peace with it.

Mariska Hargitay about Peter Hermann

Falling in love is such a force, but this is a whole other level of magic.

Alicia Keys about Swizz Beatz

At Work

- **Looking for Change**
- **Experimental**
- **Technological**

- **Focused on the Goal**
- **Team Builder**

L ooking for professional role models? Experiment like Thomas Edison (2/11/1847) until you find an effective solution. Broadcast your vision through a group like union leader John L. Lewis (2/12/1880) or IBM President Thomas Watson Sr. (2/17/1874). Leverage your popularity to help shape culture like longtime *Cosmopolitan* editor Helen Gurley Brown (2/18/1922) and television mogul Oprah Winfrey (1/29/1954).

Looking for Change

The preceding sign of Capricorn sets the societal structure; inventive Aquarius promptly wants it to change. With your view toward the future, Aquarius advocates the course of action that will move the group ahead of the times. Aquarius insists upon action as the lever of change.

He that will not apply new remedies must expect
new evils, for time is the greatest innovator.
Francis Bacon, born 1/22/1561

It is not the strongest of the species that survive, nor the
most intelligent, but the one most responsive to change.
Charles Darwin, born 2/12/1809

Things may come to those who wait, but
only the things left by those who hustle.
Abraham Lincoln, born 2/12/1809

Go West, young man, and grow up with the country.
Go West, Young Man, Go West.
Horace Greeley, born 2/3/1811

This is a world of action, and not
for moping and droning in.
Charles Dickens, born 2/7/1812

Now, here, you see, it takes all the running you can do,
to keep in the same place. If you want to get somewhere
else, you must run at least twice as fast as that.
Lewis Carroll, born 1/27/1832
Through the Looking-Glass

You don't think much of my methods. I
don't either. But I like my way of doing it
better than your way of not doing it.
Publisher D.L. Moody, born 2/5/1837

Ideas won't keep; something must be done about them.
Alfred Whitehead, born 2/15/1861

Trust only movement. Life happens at the level
of events, not of words. Trust movement.
Psychotherapist Alfred Adler, born 2/7/1870

I pledge you, I pledge myself, to a new deal for
the American people. Let us all here assembled
constitute ourselves prophets of a new order of
competence and courage. This is a call to arms.
Franklin Roosevelt, born 1/30/1882,
accepting the Presidential nomination

Because things are the way they are,
things will not stay the way they are.
Bertolt Brecht, born 2/10/1898

We must not be hampered by yesterday's
myths in concentrating on today's needs.
ITT boss Harold Geneen, born 1/22/1910

Aquarius Specialty: #1 in U.S. Presidents

Aquarius ties Scorpio for the most American Presidents (5 each out of 46). Scorpio scores due to an instinct for power; Aquarius gets the position due to the ability to communicate a vision to the American people.

Aquarius President	Birthdate	Known for:
Ronald Reagan	2/6/1911	Popularity; optimism
Franklin Roosevelt	1/30/1882	Fireside chats; New Deal
William McKinley	1/29/1843	Forging a Republican coalition
Abraham Lincoln	2/12/1809	Abolishing slavery
William Henry Harrison	2/9/1773	32-day tenure (died from pneumonia)

Without a vision, the People perish.
Franklin Roosevelt, born 1/30/1882

*To grasp and hold a vision, that is the very
essence of successful leadership—not only on the
movie set where I learned it, but everywhere.*
Ronald Reagan, born 2/6/1911

*As Reagan said, America was more than a place in the world; it
was a world-changing idea, founded on a set of principles that
had weathered many storms. Reagan restored our faith that
those principles would prove themselves again.*
Sarah Palin, born 2/11/1964

Aquarius Specialty: Union Leaders

Aquarius supports the rights of all individuals and carries an egalitarian vision of the work environment. Aquarius claims more prominent historical union leaders than any other zodiac sign.

Labor Leader	Birthdate	Known as:
Sam Gompers	1/27/1850	AFL founder
John L. Lewis	2/12/1880	President, United Mine Workers
Jimmy Hoffa	2/14/1913	Teamsters organizer

Experimental

Aquarians innovate. You try different paths as you seek the quickest road to the future. Scientist Thomas Edison (2/11/1847) epitomizes the technologically-inclined, inventive Aquarian mind with its willingness to experiment. Edison is responsible for the light bulb, phonograph and motion picture machine.

*Truth emerges more readily from
error than from confusion.*
Francis Bacon, born 1/22/1561

Oh, the joy of young ideas painted on the mind, in
the warm, glowing colors fancy spreads on objects
not yet known, when all is new and all is lovely!
                                          Hannah More, born 2/2/1745

I know that two and two make four—and should be
glad to prove it, too, if I could—though I must say
if by any sort of process I could convert two and two
into five, it would give me much greater pleasure.
                                          Lord Byron, born 1/22/1788

I love fools' experiments. I am always making them.
                                          Charles Darwin, born 2/12/1809

Towering genius disdains a beaten path.
It seeks regions hitherto unexplored.
                                          Abraham Lincoln, born 2/12/1809

After many thousand years, some man observes this long-known
effect of hot water lifting a pot-lid, and begins a train of reflection
upon it. He says, "Why, to be sure, the force that lifts the pot-lid
will lift anything else, which is no heavier than the pot-lid. And,
as man has much hard lifting to do, cannot this hot water be
made to help him?" He has become a little excited on the subject,
and he fancies he hears a voice answering "Try me."
                                          Abraham Lincoln, born 2/12/1809

I have not failed 700 times. I have not failed once. I
have succeeded in proving that those 700 ways will
not work. When I have eliminated the ways that
will not work, I will find the way that will work.
                                          Thomas Edison, born 2/11/1847

One must be a god to be able to tell successes
from failures without making a mistake.
Anton Chekhov, born 1/29/1860

If you stand up and be counted, from time to time you
may get yourself knocked down. But remember this:
A man flattened by an opponent can get up again. A
man flattened by conformity stays down for good.
IBM president Thomas Watson Sr., born 2/17/1874

The country needs and, unless I mistake its
temper, the country demands bold, persistent
experimentation. It is common sense to take a
method and try it. If it fails, admit it frankly and
try another. But above all, try something.
Franklin Roosevelt, born 1/30/1882

If you don't place your foot on the rope,
you'll never cross the chasm.
Liz Smith, born 2/2/1923

You do what you can for as long as you can,
and when you finally can't, you do the next best
thing. You back up but you don't give up.
Chuck Yeager, born 2/13/1923

The game is most fun when you are experimenting.
Jack Nicklaus, born 1/21/1940

People think that when something goes
"wrong," it's their fault. If only they had done
something differently. But sometimes things
go wrong to teach you what is right.
Alice Walker, born 2/9/1944

Think like a queen. A queen is not afraid to fail.
Failure is another steppingstone to greatness.
Oprah Winfrey, born 1/29/1954

You miss 100 percent of the shots you never take.
Wayne Gretzky, born 1/26/1961

Technological

Aquarians are the inventors and early adopters. Aquarians gravitate to the latest wave of technology be it aviation, computers or Kindles. Aquarius contributed leaders to IBM, Xerox, SONY and Microsoft as these companies forged ahead with technological advancement.

"What sort of things do you remember
best?" Alice ventured to ask. "Oh, things
that happened the week after next."
Lewis Carroll, born 1/27/1832

The greatest task before civilization at present
is to make machines what they ought to be,
the slaves, instead of the masters of men.
Havelock Ellis, born 2/2/1859

It is the business of the future to be dangerous.
Alfred Whitehead, born 2/15/1861

Even if smog were a risk to human life, we
must remember that life in nature, without
technology, is wholesale death.
Ayn Rand, born 2/2/1905

*I'm a geek, and I spend a lot of time on the
computer. I build Web sites, and I'm always
getting e-mail and fixing computers.*

Alan Alda, born 1/28/1936

*It is not enough to wire the world if you short-circuit
the soul. Technology without heart is not enough.*

Tom Brokaw, born 2/6/1940

*I wish I was better at doing the robot. It's just a skill I
think everyone should study, understand and acquire.
You need to really know how to embody a robot.*

Glee star Heather Morris, born 2/1/1987

Aquarius Specialty: Aviation

Aquarians relish the freedom and perspective of flight. Charles Lindbergh (2/4/1902) accomplished the first transatlantic flight, and Chuck Yeager (2/13/1923) remains the most famous test pilot of all time. World War II fliers include Clark Gable (2/1/1901) and Jack Palance (2/18/1919).

*Science, freedom, beauty, adventure.
What more could you ask of life? Aviation
combined all the elements I loved.*

Charles Lindbergh, born 2/4/1902

In developing aviation, in making it a form of commerce, in replacing the wild freedom of danger with the civilized bonds of safety, must we give up this miracle of the air? Will men fly through the sky in the future without seeing what I have seen, without feeling what I have felt? Is that true of all things we call progress—Do the gods retire as commerce and science advance?

Charles Lindbergh, born 2/4/1902

The earth was falling downward, and she felt
as if its weight were dropping off her ankles, as
if the globe would go shrinking to the size of a
ball, a convict's ball she had dragged and lost.

Ayn Rand, born 2/2/1905
Atlas Shrugged

Anyone that tells you that having your own
private jet isn't great is lying to you.

Oprah Winfrey, born 1/29/1954

It was the wonder of flight. It was the design of the aircraft;
they made my heart pound, the way they looked. I get almost
a romantic feeling about that. Who was on board? Weren't
they lucky to be going someplace? Anywhere would have been
exciting, as long as they were in a plane.

John Travolta, born 2/18/1954

Every age needs men who will redeem the time
by living with a vision of things that are to be.

Adlai Stevenson, born 2/5/1900

Focused on the Goal

From your vantage point in the skies, Aquarians see farther than others. You set the long-range goal, then keep your eyes on the horizon so that the group stays focused. Aquarius serves as keeper of the vision.

Men, like snails, lose their usefulness when
they lose direction and begin to bend.

Walter Savage Landor, born 1/30/1775

Determine that the thing can and shall
be done and then find the way.

Abraham Lincoln, born 2/12/1809

One day Alice came to a fork in the road and saw a Cheshire cat
in a tree.
"Which road do I take?" she asked.
"Where do you want to go?" was his response.
"I don't know," Alice answered.
"Then," said the cat, "it doesn't matter."

Lewis Carroll, born 1/27/1832
Alice in Wonderland

If you cry "Forward!" you must without fail
make it plain in what direction to go. Don't
you see that if, without doing so, you call out
the word to both a monk and a revolutionary,
they will go in directions precisely opposite?

Anton Chekhov, born 1/29/1860

Convictions no doubt have to be modified or
expanded to meet changing conditions but . . . to
be a reliable political leader sooner or later your
anchors must hold fast where other men's drag.

Margot Asquith, born 2/2/1864

If you want to be a big company tomorrow,
you have to start acting like one today.

Thomas Watson Sr., born 2/17/1874

We need to learn to set our course by the stars,
not by the lights of every passing ship.

Omar Bradley, born 2/12/1893

My coach always taught me not to get
caught up in the emotion of the moment, but
to keep my eye on the bigger picture.
Mary Lou Retton, born 1/24/1968

Team Builder

Aquarian managers build effective teams. Aquarius communicates clear group objectives before delegating responsibility to the ones doing the work.

In order that people may be happy in their
work, these three things are needed: They must
be fit for it. They must not do too much of it.
And they must have a sense of success in it.
John Ruskin, born 2/8/1819

I consider my ability to arouse enthusiasm
among men the greatest asset I possess.
Industrialist Charles Schwab, born 2/18/1862

My most important contribution to IBM was my ability to pick
strong and intelligent men and then hold the team together by
persuasion, by apologies, by financial incentives, by speeches,
by chatting with their wives, by thoughtfulness when they were
sick . . . and by using every tool at my command to make that
team think I was a decent guy.
Thomas J. Watson, born 2/17/1874

I make the decision, and then turn the job over to
a cabinet member and leave him or her alone.
Franklin Roosevelt, born 1/30/1882

*Surround yourself with the best people you can
find, delegate authority, and don't interfere.*
Ronald Reagan, born 2/6/1911

*If you've done well, it's your responsibility
to send the elevator back down.*
Jack Lemmon, born 2/8/1925

*During the 1968-69 season, my last as a player and a coach
for the Celtics, we won only 48 regular-season games, a sharp
decline from where we had been in previous years. But something
special happened, as it often did, when we got into the playoffs.
That's when Celtic Pride started shining through again. The
talents of each player were channeled for the benefit of the team,
not for any statistics or individual awards. Simply put, our entire
organization, from the owner down to the man who swept the
locker room, had the same unspoken understanding: We knew
our sole purpose as an organization was to win. I call it team
ego.*
Bill Russell, born 2/12/1934

*Everybody talks about unconditional love. My love has some
conditions. I showed you my love for you by providing you a
home, by providing somebody to take care of you, putting you
in private schools . . . So this is the condition: You have to give
me what I've given you. I've given you my best, and that's what
I want from you. I want your best.*
Oprah Winfrey, born 1/29/1954,
to first class at a new school she opened in Africa

Aquarius Politicians

Aquarius contributes the following political leaders in addition to the U.S. Presidents and union leaders already named.

Aquarius Politician	Birthdate	Position:
Abdullah II	1/30/1962	King of Jordan
Princess Caroline	1/23/1957	Royal family of Monaco
Nicolas Sarkozy	1/28/1955	French President
Jeb Bush	2/11/1953	Florida governor
Dan Quayle	2/4/1947	U.S. Vice President
Isayas Afewerki	2/2/1945	Eritrea dictator
Michael Bloomberg	2/14/1942	New York City mayor
Ehud Barak	2/12/1942	Israeli prime minister
Kim Jong-il	2/16/1941	North Korean dictator
Dick Cheney	1/30/1941	U.S. Vice President
Corazon Aquino	1/25/1933	People Power (Philippines)
Boris Yeltsin	2/1/1931	Russian leader
Chuck Yeager	2/13/1923	Brigadier General
Nicolae Ceausescu	1/26/1918	Romanian dictator
U Thant	1/22/1909	UN Secretary-General
Anastasio Somoza Garcia	2/1/1896	Nicaraguan dictator
Roger Baldwin	1/21/1884	Founder of the ACLU
Douglas MacArthur	1/26/1880	American General
Aaron Burr	2/6/1756	U.S. Senator / Vice President
Frederick the Great	1/24/1712	King of Prussia

Aquarius Business Leaders

Aquarius Leader	Birthdate	Known as:
Paul Allen	1/21/1953	Microsoft co-founder
Helen Gurley Brown	2/18/1922	Longtime Cosmopolitan editor
Akio Morita	1/26/1921	SONY chairman
Harold Geneen	1/22/1910	Longtime ITT leader

William Levitt	2/11/1907	Father of modern suburbia
Thomas Watson Sr.	2/17/1874	IBM President
Charles Schwab	2/18/1862	Steel industry executive
Bernard Kroger	1/24/1860	Kroger supermarkets creator
Aaron Montgomery Ward	2/17/1843	Mail order pioneer

*Management manages by making decisions and
by seeing that those decisions are implemented.*
Harold Geneen, born 1/22/1910

Aquarius Scientists

Aquarius Scientist	Birthdate	Discovery / Invention
Fritjof Capra	2/1/1939	Environmentalism
Chester Carlson	2/8/1906	Xerography (copying process)
Irving Langmuir	1/31/1881	Atomic structure
David Hilbert	1/23/1862	Foundation of geometry
Thomas Edison	2/11/1847	Light bulb, phonograph, etc.
Cyrus McCormick	2/15/1809	Mechanical reaper on large scale
Charles Darwin	2/12/1809	Evolution theory
John Fitch	1/21/1743	Steamship (20 years before Fulton)

*Not only will atomic power be released, but
someday we will harness the rise and fall of
the tides and imprison the rays of the sun.*
Thomas Edison, born 2/11/1847

Creativity

Aquarian Mozart remains the most revered composer of all time. James Joyce and Virginia Woolf literally poured the Aquarian wellspring into stream-of-consciousness narrative. Novels from Aquarians Charles Dickens, Sinclair Lewis and Toni Morrison expose social injustice. Today's cinema rests upon the experimental techniques of early Aquarian filmmakers D.W. Griffith and John Ford.

- Detached
- Experimental
- Innovative

- Popular
- Sometimes Silly

Detached

Only an indirect method is effective. We do nothing if we have not first drawn back.
Simone Weil, born 2/3/1909

The Aquarian artist needs space. The Water-Bearer insists upon enough separation to grasp the whole picture. Aquarian detachment adds perspective to your creative product.

To a chemist nothing on earth is unclean. A writer must be as objective as a chemist; he must abandon the subjective line; he must know that dung-heaps play a very respectable part in a landscape, and that evil passions are as inherent in life as good ones.
Anton Chekhov, born 1/29/1860

There are two ways of spreading light: to be
The candle or the mirror that reflects it.
Edith Wharton, born 1/24/1862
Vesalius in Zante

Everybody gets so much information all day
long that they lose their common sense.
Gertrude Stein, born 2/3/1874

I am extremely happy walking on the downs. I
like to have space to spread my mind out in.
Virginia Woolf, born 1/25/1882

The artist, like the God of the creation, remains within or behind or beyond or above his handiwork, invisible, refined out of existence, indifferent, paring his fingernails.
James Joyce, born 2/2/1882
A Portrait of the Artist as a Young Man

A work of art has an author and yet,
when it is perfect, it has something which
is essentially anonymous about it.
Simone Weil, born 2/3/1909
Gravity and Grace

The She-Wolf came into existence because I had to paint it. Any attempt on my part to say something about it, to attempt any explanation of the inexplicable, could only destroy it.

Jackson Pollock, born 1/28/1912

I need to be able to see great distances clear to the horizon for one thing, and also have a lot of time that is quiet and pure, in which there is no noise or bills to pay. It's just very important to have a space that is really, really clear for whatever is emerging to come.

Alice Walker, born 2/9/1944

Experimental

The Capricorn artist finds and repeats a successful formula, while Aries tries a different genre for the excitement of a new challenge. The Aquarian artist experiments for the sake of experimentation. More than any other sign, Aquarian artists talk about consciously changing style. You try a new process because you want to see if it works. Aquarian experimentation often provides the breakthrough that moves artistic tradition to a new level.

*To be a leader of men, one must
turn one's back on men.*

Havelock Ellis, born 2/2/1859

*I have no fears of making changes, destroying
the image, etc., because the painting has a life
of its own. I try to let it come through.*

Jackson Pollock, born 1/28/1912

My novels are all different. It isn't like when you read one Hemingway novel you know a lot about the other Hemingway novels, whether you read them or not. My novels are all over the place.

Norman Mailer, born 1/31/1923

I have a very mercurial character as an artist, and I can't keep repeating one pattern. I'll be doing something, and then I get a totally different idea and jump to that.

Yoko Ono, born 2/18/1933

My appetite is to do different things. I kind of like to push the edges.

Tom Selleck, born 1/29/1945

We have to keep trying things we're not sure we can pull off. If we just do the things we know we can do . . . you don't grow as much. You gotta take those chances on making those big mistakes.

Cybill Shepherd, born 2/18/1950

We just went out and we done it in front of the public. We didn't stay in a rehearsal studio until we were so perfect we were boring. The whole idea was to get out and have some fun and we hoped that someone out there would see us and have fun, too. We just wanted to get out and play and we hoped that some people would see us and go away and form their own bands. We wanted to make a new scene.

Johnny Rotten, born 1/31/1956

I don't want to do the same stuff over and over.

Ashton Kutcher, born 2/7/1978

Aquarius Specialty: Literary Experimentation

- Charles Dickens (2/7/1812) experimented with letters as the narrative structure in *The Pickwick Papers*

- James Joyce (2/2/1882) used neither plot nor characters. His novel *Ulysses* brings stream-of-consciousness narrative to its highest level.

- Virginia Woolf (1/25/1882) applied the new stream-of-consciousness techniques to her novels *Mrs. Dalloway* and *To the Lighthouse*

> *A man of genius makes no mistakes. His errors are volitional and are the portals of discovery.*
> James Joyce, born 2/2/1882
> Ulysses

> *I have been the creative literary mind of the century.*
> Gertrude Stein, born 2/3/1874

Innovative

The self-centered Uranus of myth was castrated by his children to allow succession to the throne. The seed of Uranus scattered into the sea and led to the birth of Venus, goddess of the arts. From destruction comes creativity. Several Aquarian artists express the willingness to destroy so that new forms can emerge.

> *The artist must possess the courageous soul that dares and defies.*
> Kate Chopin, born 2/8/1850

> *But an author is one who can judge his own stuff's worth, without pity, and destroy most of it.*
> Colette, born 1/28/1873

My views are not yet part of the history
of philosophy, but they will be.

Ayn Rand, born 2/2/1905,
response to an early philosophy professor

The people who say you are not facing reality actually mean that you are not facing their idea of reality. Reality is above all else a variable, and nobody is qualified to say that he or she knows exactly what it is. As a matter of fact, with a firm enough commitment, you can sometimes create a reality which did not exist before.

Margaret Halsey, born 2/13/1910

On the floor I am more at ease. I feel nearer,
more a part of the painting, since in this way
I can walk around it, work from the four
sides and literally be in the painting.

Jackson Pollock, born 1/28/1912

Almost all of the African-American women writers that I know were very much uninterested in one area: white men . . . the establishment. The reviewers. The publishers. The people who are in control. Once you erase that from your canvas, you can really play.

Toni Morrison, born 2/18/1931

Be brave enough to live creatively. The creative is the place where no one else has ever been. You have to leave the city of your comfort and go into the wilderness of your intuition. What you will discover will be wonderful. What you will discover will be yourself.

Alan Alda, born 1/28/1936

140

*I love the term "outlaw," as long as it applies
strictly to the music. I like having music that is
a little bit different from everybody else's, and I
think that's what the term "outlaw" implies.*
Travis Tritt, born 2/9/1963

*I have failed over and over again in my
life. And that is why I succeed.*
Michael Jordan, born 2/17/1963

*I created the part for myself. If there's not
a part for you, create your own.*
Minnie Driver, born 1/31/1970,
cast as a tree in school play but played a fairy

*We want to create the hot new thing. If we can't keep
it new, we're not going to do it. That's our philosophy.*
Ashton Kutcher, born 2/7/1978,
about his MTV hit Punk'd

Aquarius Specialty: Artistic Innovation

- Composer Mozart (1/27/1756) mixed graceful, light sound with darkness and passion
- Edouard Manet (1/23/1832) broke tradition by displaying *The Fifer* against a blank background
- Manet's *The Luncheon on the Grass* mimicked a traditional masterpiece with participants now disengaged from the scene
- Jackson Pollock (1/28/1912) used different ways of applying paint to different surfaces
- Oprah (1/27/1954) proved that popular talk shows can grapple with social issues

Neither a lofty degree of intelligence nor imagination
nor both together go to the making of genius.
Love, love, love, that is the soul of genius.
Wolfgang Amadeus Mozart, born 1/27/1756

Aquarius Specialty: #1 in Director Oscars

Technologically-inclined, visionary Aquarius took naturally to film as the new medium emerged. Russian director Sergei
Eisenstein (1/23/1898) introduced film montage, while D.W. Griffith
(1/22/1875) pioneered different camera angles, film time, and the
musical score. Aquarian film directors have earned more Academy
Awards than any other sign of the zodiac.

Oscar-Winning Director	Birthdate	Movie
Michael Cimino	2/3/1939	The Deer Hunter
Milos Forman	2/18/1932	Amadeus
Milos Forman	2/18/1932	One Flew Over the Cuckoo's Nest
John Schlesinger	2/16/1926	Midnight Cowboy
Delbert Mann	1/30/1920	Marty
Joseph Mankiewicz	2/11/1909	Letter to Three Wives
Joseph Mankiewicz	2/11/1909	All About Eve
John Ford	2/1/1895	The Informer
John Ford	2/1/1895	How Green Was My Valley
John Ford	2/1/1895	The Quiet Man
John Ford	2/1/1895	The Grapes of Wrath
Frank Lloyd	2/2/1886	The Divine Lady
Frank Lloyd	2/2/1886	Cavalcade

Popular

I'm grateful to have been the guy in that box [of superstardom]. But I don't want to go there again.
Tom Selleck, born 1/29/1945

Famous Aquarians enjoy uncanny mass appeal. Ronald Reagan was America's most popular President. Some Aquarian celebrities like Burt Reynolds, Paris Hilton and Wilmer Valderrama go through a period as the media's #1 all-star before fading to relative obscurity. Aquarians celebrities like Jennifer Aniston, Garth Brooks, John Travolta and Oprah reach a transcendent popularity where they can do no wrong. Mass media make Aquarius the most liked sign of the zodiac.

Public opinion is everything. With public sentiment nothing can fail; without it, nothing can succeed. Consequently, he who molds public opinion goes deeper than he who enacts statutes or pronounces decisions.
Abraham Lincoln, born 2/12/1809

I almost wish I hadn't gone down that rabbit hole; and yet—and yet—it's rather curious you know, this sort of life! I do wonder what can have happened to me! When I used to read fairy tales I fancied that kind of thing never happened, and now here I am in the middle of one!
Lewis Carroll, born 1/27/1832
Alice in Wonderland

I'd been the number one star in the world and I was the only guy to go from number one to number 138. That's when you reach down and find out whether you've got any balls.
Burt Reynolds, born 2/11/1936

*I really don't like to think about it. If I try to
evaluate my appeal, I'm afraid I may become self-
conscious and lose it. Better to just let it be.*

Tom Selleck, born 1/29/1945

*Coming out on the show proved to be a huge success. We had 46
million viewers. People held parties around the country to watch.
It became a cultural event. My heart felt good. Many people have
told me that they came out after watching that show with their
parents.*

Ellen DeGeneres, born 1/26/1958

*Because I don't know why it works, I don't
know why they're so sweet to me.*

Garth Brooks, born 2/7/1962,
about why he gets nervous before performing

*Since being elected governor in 2006, I had managed
to rack up an 88 percent approval rating, and though
I didn't put much stock in fickle polls, I figured my
administration must be doing something right.*

Sarah Palin, born 2/11/1964

*I liken myself to Oprah. I'm gonna take the high
road, talk about stuff that's interesting. So even if
you don't think I'm funny, I'm not boring you.*

Chris Rock, born 2/7/1965

*Her character does things that are not very nice, [but] we forgive
her. That's a quality that's rare among actors. [Aquarian] Jack
Lemmon had it; we let him sin and then redeem himself . . . But
women, as a rule, are not afforded the opportunity, or we don't
recognize it as quickly in them. It's a great gift that she has.*

Director Glenn Caron about Jennifer Aniston, born 2/11/1969

144

I realized there was nothing gained by playing small to make others feel comfortable. Who was I to deny myself the light within me, the light that is within everyone? We all need to celebrate who we are and what we have to give to the world . . . I realized that I did have a value and a place in the world, and part of that was making people laugh on a grand scale. Making lots and lots of people laugh, people I would never know, but perhaps people who needed to laugh. Now I'm grateful for my achievements and happy in giving what I have to offer as a human being.

Jennifer Aniston, born 2/11/1969

Sometimes Silly

Intellectual Aquarius can surprise with silliness. Promotional gags from baseball promoter Bill Veeck (2/9/1914) ranged from clowns in the coaching box to a dwarf as pinch hitter. Famous Aquarian comedians include W.C. Fields, Jimmy Durante, Jack Benny and Chris Rock. The unplanned solo dance by Ellen DeGeneres (1/26/1958) as she opened a show has become a staple of daytime television. "All I Wanna Do Is Have Some Fun" is the apt title of the biggest hit from Sheryl Crow (2/11/1962).

It is requisite for the relaxation of the mind that we make use, from time to time, of playful deeds and jokes.

Thomas Aquinas, born 1/28/1225

The sublime and the ridiculous are often so nearly related, that it is difficult to class them separately. One step above the sublime, makes the ridiculous; and one step above the ridiculous, makes the sublime again.

Thomas Paine, born 2/9/1737

There might be some credit in being jolly.

Charles Dickens, born 2/7/1812

Don't you think they overdo it? And are human laborers to have no holidays, because of the bees? And am I never to have change of air, because the bees don't? Mr. Boffin, I think honey excellent at breakfast; but regarded in the light of my conventional schoolmaster and moralist, I protest against the tyrannical humbug of your friend the bee. With the highest respect for you.

Charles Dickens, born 2/7/1812
Our Mutual Friend

Beware the Jabberwock, my son!
The jaws that bite, the claws that catch!
Beware the Jubjub bird, and shun
The frumious Bandersnatch!

Lewis Carroll, born 1/27/1832

Come forth, Lazarus! And he came
fifth and lost the job.

James Joyce, born 2/2/1882
Ulysses

Once you've seen your face on a bottle of salad
dressing, it's hard to take yourself seriously.

Paul Newman, born 1/26/1925

If he [Al Gore] invented the Internet,
I invented spellcheck.

Dan Quayle, born 2/4/1947

I've always used humor to lighten the
mood. That's how I deal with things.

Larry the Cable Guy, born 2/17/1963

I'm so sick of the tortured-artist thing. High
art comes from having a good time.

Laura Dern, born 2/1/1967

Aquarius Visual Artists

Well-known contributors to Western art history include the following Aquarians:

Aquarius Painter	Birthdate	Known for:
Jackson Pollock	1/28/1912	Abstractions
Norman Rockwell	2/3/1894	Everyday American life
Max Beckmann	2/12/1884	German painter and sculptor
Fernand Léger	2/4/1881	Figurative cubism
Edouard Manet	1/23/1832	The Fifer
Charles Daubigny	2/15/1817	French Impressionist
Henry Fuseli	2/7/1741	Wild animals
Guercino	2/8/1591	Drawings

Abstract painting is abstract. It confronts you. There was a reviewer a while back who wrote that my pictures didn't have any beginning or any end. He didn't mean it as a compliment but it was. It was a fine compliment. Only he didn't know it.

Jackson Pollock, born 1/28/1912

Aquarius Architect	Birthdate	Known for:
Eugene Viollet-le-Duc	1/28/1814	Gothic Revival
François Mansart	1/23/1598	Mansard roof

Aquarius Cartoonist	Birthdate	Known for:
Matt Groening	2/15/1954	The Simpsons
Johnny Hart	2/18/1931	B.C.

Basically, everything I try to do is to present an alternative to what somebody else is doing.

Matt Groening, born 2/15/1954

Aquarius Designer	Birthdate	Known for:
Christian Dior	1/21/1905	High-fashion lines
Cristobal Balenciaga	1/21/1895	Tunic and Empire-waist dresses
Louis Tiffany	2/18/1848	Stained glass

Aquarius Writers

This list includes recent popular novelists and classic writers typically covered in collegiate literature studies.

Aquarius Writer	Birthdate	Known for:
John Grisham	2/8/1955	Popular thrillers
Alice Walker	2/9/1944	The Color Purple
Judy Blume	2/12/1938	Preteen fiction
Jean Auel	2/18/1936	The Clan of the Cave Bear
Toni Morrison	2/18/1931	Beloved
Judith Viorst	2/2/1931	Children's literature
Chaim Potok	2/17/1929	Jewish themes
Brendan Behan	2/9/1923	Irish poems and plays
Betty Friedan	2/4/1921	The Feminine Mystique
Sidney Shelton	2/11/1917	Popular novels
Elizabeth Bishop	2/8/1911	Poetry
James Michener	2/3/1907	Historical sagas
Ayn Rand	2/2/1905	Atlas Shrugged
Langston Hughes	2/1/1902	African-American poetry
Bertolt Brecht	2/10/1898	The Threepenny Opera
Sinclair Lewis	2/7/1885	The Jungle
James Joyce	2/2/1882	Ulysses
Virginia Woolf	1/25/1882	Mrs. Dalloway
Zane Grey	1/31/1875	Riders of the Purple Sage
Amy Lowell	2/9/1874	What's O'Clock
Gertrude Stein	2/3/1874	The Autobiography of Alice B. Toklas
W. Somerset Maugham	1/25/1874	Of Human Bondage

Colette	1/28/1873	Earthly Paradise
Edith Wharton	1/24/1862	Age of Innocence
Kate Chopin	2/8/1850	The Awakening
Henry Adams	2/16/1838	The Education of Henry Adams
Lewis Carroll	1/27/1832	Alice in Wonderland
Jules Verne	2/8/1828	Space, air and underwater travel
Charles Dickens	2/7/1812	Oliver Twist
Horace Greeley	2/3/1811	Newspaper editor
Lydia Child	2/11/1802	19th-century issues
Lord Byron	1/22/1788	Romantic poetry
Stendhal	1/23/1783	The Red and the Black
Charles Lamb	2/10/1775	Essays of Elia
Robert Burns	1/25/1759	Scottish poetry
Thomas Paine	2/9/1737	Common Sense
Pierre Beaumarchais	1/24/1732	Barber of Seville
William Congreve	1/24/1670	Lesbia
Madame de Sévigné	2/5/1626	Letters
Francis Bacon	1/22/1561	Essays
Thomas More	2/7/1478	Utopia

There are three rules for writing the novel.
Unfortunately, no one knows what they are.

W. Somerset Maugham, born 1/25/1874

Aquarius Composers

Famous Aquarian composers have been unusually prolific.

Aquarius Composer	Birthdate	Known for:
Philip Glass	1/31/1937	Music with repetitive structures
Alban Berg	2/9/1885	Romanticism-Expressionism bridge
Jerome Kern	1/27/1885	Showboat; show tunes
Eubie Blake	2/7/1883	Boogie-woogie pioneer, almost 1000 songs

Felix Mendelssohn	2/3/1809	A Midsummer Night's Dream
Franz Schubert	1/31/1797	Unfinished Symphony
Wolfgang Amadeus Mozart	1/27/1756	More than 600 compositions
Arcangelo Corelli	2/7/1653	Baroque sonatas

I cannot write in verse, for I am no poet. I cannot arrange the parts of speech with such art as to produce effects of light and shade, for I am no painter. Even by signs and gestures I cannot express my thoughts and feelings, for I am no dancer. But I can do so by means of sounds, for I am a musician.

Wolfgang Amadeus Mozart, born 1/27/1756

I am in the world only for the purpose of composing.

Franz Schubert, born 1/31/1797

Aquarius Grammys

The most prestigious Grammys are awarded for Album, Record and Song of the Year. Song of the Year goes to the composer, often unknown except within the music industry. This Grammy list includes only those Aquarians awarded with Album or Record of the Year. Aquarius members of winning music groups are listed when holding a prominent position in the group. (Go to www.QuotableZodiac. com for astrological updates on all annual entertainment awards.)

Aquarius Musician	Birthdate	Record / Album
Big Boi (OutKast)	2/1/1975	Speakerboxxx/The Love Below
Billie Joe Armstrong (Green Day)	2/17/1972	Boulevard of Broken Dreams
Rob Thomas (with Santana)	2/14/1972	Smooth
Sheryl Crow	2/11/1962	All I Wanna Do
Michael McDonald (Doobie Bros.)	2/12/1952	What a Fool Believes
Phil Collins	1/30/1951	Another Day in Paradise

Phil Collins	1/30/1951	No Jacket Required
Natalie Cole (with Nat King Cole)	2/6/1950	Unforgettable
Carole King	2/9/1942	Tapestry
Carole King	2/9/1942	It's Too Late
Roberta Flack	2/10/1937	Killing Me Softly with His Song
Roberta Flack	2/10/1937	First Time Ever I Saw Your Face
Yoko Ono (with Lennon)	2/18/1933	Double Fantasy
Stan Getz	2/2/1927	The Girl from Ipanema
Stan Getz	2/2/1927	Getz/Gilberto

We never try and reinvent the past. We try to look forward to what's going on . . . We don't have a set plan—you might have ideas, or a different set pieces you might use to put inside your puzzle—but it's like you always have to look forward to what's beyond from where you just came from.

Big Boi, born 2/1/1975

Contemporary Aquarius Musicians

Aquarius Pop / Rock	Birthdate	Known for:
Adam Lambert	1/29/1982	Outrageous appearance
Justin Timberlake	1/31/1981	Future Sex/Love Sounds
Alicia Keys	1/25/1981	The Diary of Alicia Keys
Nick Carter	1/28/1980	Backstreet Boys
Brandy	2/11/1979	Singer-songwriter and actress
Shakira	2/2/1977	Hips Don't Lie
Joey Fatone	1/28/1977	'N Sync
Natalie Imbruglia	2/4/1975	Torn
Sarah McLachlan	1/28/1968	Emotional ballads
Robert DeLeo	2/2/1966	Stone Temple Pilots
David Bryan	2/7/1962	Bon Jovi
Axl Rose	2/6/1962	Guns 'N Roses

Eddie Van Halen	1/26/1957	Jump
Johnny Rotten	1/31/1956	Sex Pistols
Alice Cooper	2/4/1948	School's Out
Mick Avory	2/15/1944	The Kinks
Carole King	2/9/1942	Tapestry
Neil Diamond	1/24/1941	Cracklin' Rosie
Roberta Flack	2/10/1937	Killing Me Softly

*The sense of community. That feeling of
being surrounded by empathy, love, trust
and compassion is so important.*
Sarah McLachlan, born 1/28/1968,
on why she revived the Lilith tour

Aquarius Country	Birthdate	Known for:
Travis Tritt	2/9/1963	It's All About to Change
Garth Brooks	2/7/1962	Top seller in U.S. music history
Clint Black	2/4/1962	Killin' Time
Tennessee Ernie Ford	2/13/1919	Sixteen Tons

*The thing I love the most about country music
is that it can give you the sales you can have in
every format, and, at the same time, you come off
that stage, they treat you like an average Joe.*
Garth Brooks, born 2/7/1962

Rap / Hip-Hop	Birthdate	Known for:
Big Boi	2/1/1975	OutKast
Dr. Dre	2/8/1965	Let Me Ride

Classical / Jazz	Birthdate	Known for:
Natalie Cole	2/6/1950	Unforgettable
Placido Domingo	1/21/1941	Versatile operatic voice

Stan Getz	2/2/1927	The Girl from Ipanema
Leontyne Price	2/10/1927	Soprano / opera

> *For a long time the only time I felt beautiful—in the*
> *sense of being complete as a woman, as a human*
> *being, and even female—was when I was singing.*
>
> Leontyne Price, born 2/10/1927

Aquarius Specialty: #2 in Actor Oscars

Oscars for outstanding film achievement have been awarded each year since 1928. The following actor and actress lists include Aquarian winners in both lead and supporting roles. Popular Aquarius ties sensitive Cancer for #2 in actor Oscars behind confident, aggressive Aries.

Oscar-Winning Actor	Birthdate	Movie
Joe Pesci	2/9/1943	Goodfellas
Gene Hackman	1/30/1931	Unforgiven
Gene Hackman	1/30/1931	The French Connection
George Kennedy	2/18/1925	Cool Hand Luke
Jack Lemmon	2/8/1925	Save the Tiger
Jack Lemmon	2/8/1925	Mister Roberts
Paul Newman	1/26/1925	The Color of Money
Paul Scofield	1/21/1922	A Man for All Seasons
Jack Palance	2/18/1919	City Slickers
Red Buttons	2/5/1919	Sayonara
Ernest Borgnine	1/24/1917	Marty
Clark Gable	2/1/1901	It Happened One Night
Humphrey Bogart	1/23/1899	The African Queen
Ronald Colman	2/9/1891	A Double Life

Being an actor is the loneliest thing in the
world. You are all alone with your concentration
and imagination, and that's all you have.

James Dean, born 2/8/1931

Aquarius Specialty: Last in Actress Oscars

Cool, intellectual Aquarius has earned fewer actress Oscars than any other astrological sign.

Oscar-Winning Actress	Birthdate	Movie
Geena Davis	1/21/1956	The Accidental Tourist
Mary Steenburgen	2/8/1953	Melvin & Howard
Brenda Fricker	2/17/1945	My Left Foot
Vanessa Redgrave	1/30/1937	Julia
Dorothy Malone	1/30/1925	Written on the Wind
Donna Reed	1/27/1921	From Here to Eternity
Gale Sondergaard	2/15/1899	Anthony Adverse

I look for roles that break the mold, both because
I want to do the fun stuff and because I want to
play roles women can enjoy and feel good about.

Geena Davis, born 1/21/1956

I don't like to look beautiful. I want to change.

Ziyi Zhang, born 2/9/1979

Aquarius Roles and Productions

- D.W. Griffith (1/22/1875) made movies about Aquarians Abraham Lincoln and Charles Darwin
- Micawber in *David Copperfield* by Aquarian Charles Dickens was the only serious film role from W.C. Fields (1/29/1880)
- W.C. Fields played Humpty Dumpty in the film adaptation of *Alice in Wonderland* by Aquarian Lewis Carroll

- Aquarian Ronald Reagan (2/6/1911) played Aquarian football player George Gipp (2/8/1895) in the movie *Knute Rockne: All-American*
- Aquarian Paul Scofield (1/21/1922) earned an Oscar for playing Aquarian Thomas More (2/7/1478) in *A Man for All Seasons*
- The movie *Amadeus* by Milos Forman (2/18/1932) was about Aquarian composer Mozart (1/27/1756)
- Milos Forman directed *Hair* welcoming the Age of Aquarius
- Oprah (1/27/1954) starred in *The Color Purple* by Aquarian Alice Walker
- Oprah played Sethe in *Beloved* by Aquarian Toni Morrison

> *I kept getting stuck on those first eight pages. I told Toni it was hard to get through, that I had to work, and she said, "It's called reading, dear."*
> Oprah Winfrey, born 1/29/1954,
> about Toni Morrison's Beloved

Aquarius Emmys

The annual Emmy Awards recognize excellence on television. With lead and supporting honors in drama, comedy, miniseries and guest appearances, almost 1,000 acting Emmys have been awarded since 1949. Outstanding performances often receive consecutive awards as a television series continues its run. So the following lists include only multiple winners—Aquarians who won at least two Emmy awards either on different programs or with repeated honors for the same role.

Emmy-Winning Actress	Birthdate	Show(s)
Laura Linney	2/5/1964	Specials
Stockard Channing	2/13/1944	The West Wing, special
Blythe Danner	2/3/1943	Huff
Vanessa Redgrave	1/30/1937	Specials
Elaine Stritch	2/2/1925	Variety, guest appearance
Judith Anderson	2/10/1897	Macbeth (2x)

[Playing Olivia Benson] fulfills me as an artist
and rewards me even more as a human being.
It is powerful and life-affirming to extend my
hand and my heart to those who are in need.

Mariska Hargitay, born 1/23/1964,
about her Emmy-winning role on Law & Order: SVU

Emmy-Winning Actor	Birthdate	Show(s)
James Spader	2/7/1960	The Practice, Boston Legal
Charles Dutton	1/30/1951	Guest appearances
Stuart Margolin	1/31/1940	The Rockford Files
Alan Alda	1/28/1936	M*A*S*H
Hal Holbrook	2/17/1925	Specials

Hollywood's Aquarius A-Listers

Contemporary musicians and the Aquarius award winners already named obviously qualify for the entertainment world's A list. In addition, these Aquarius celebrities make headlines for just about anything they do.

Aquarius Celebrity	Birthdate	Known for:
Freddie Highmore	2/14/1992	Finding Neverland
Taylor Lautner	2/11/1992	Twilight Saga film series
Emma Roberts	2/10/1991	Hotel for Dogs

Darren Criss	2/5/1987	Glee
Amber Riley	2/15/1986	Glee
Lauren Conrad	2/1/1986	The Hills
Mischa Barton	1/24/1986	The O.C.
Athina Onassis	1/29/1985	Heiress
Camila Alves	1/28/1982	Partner of Matt McConaughey
Paris Hilton	2/17/1981	Socialite headlines
Elijah Wood	1/28/1981	The Lord of the Rings
Christina Ricci	2/12/1980	Grey's Anatomy / Pan Am
Wilmer Valderrama	1/30/1980	That '70s Show
Ziyi Zhang	2/9/1979	Crouching Tiger, Hidden Dragon
Ashton Kutcher	2/7/1978	That '70s Show / Punk'd
Kerry Washington	1/31/1977	Ray
Isla Fisher	2/3/1976	Wedding Crashers
Balthazar Getty	1/22/1975	Brothers and Sisters
Jerry O'Connell	2/17/1974	Scream 2
Ed Helms	1/24/1974	The Office
Portia de Rossi	1/31/1973	Ally McBeal, Arrested Development
Denise Richards	2/17/1972	The World Is Not Enough
Michael C. Hall	2/1/1971	Dexter, Six Feet Under
Gabrielle Anwar	2/4/1970	The Tudors
Jennifer Aniston	2/11/1969	Friends; movies
Josh Brolin	2/12/1968	No Country for Old Men
Lisa Marie Presley	2/1/1968	Elvis' daughter
Laura Dern	2/1/1967	Rambling Rose
Chris Rock	2/7/1965	No-holds-barred comedy
Maura Tierney	2/3/1965	ER
Diane Lane	1/22/1965	Unfaithful
Matt Dillon	2/18/1964	Crash
Mariska Hargitay	1/23/1964	Law & Order: SVU
Larry the Cable Guy	2/17/1963	Comedy; TV series
Carey Lowell	2/11/1961	Law & Order

Anthony LaPaglia	1/31/1959	Without a Trace
Ice-T	2/16/1958	Law & Order: SVU
Arsenio Hall	2/12/1958	Talk show host
Ellen DeGeneres	1/26/1958	Ellen; daily talk show
John Travolta	2/18/1954	Grease, Saturday Night Fever
Christie Brinkley	2/2/1954	Model
Oprah Winfrey	1/29/1954	Talk show
Jane Seymour	2/15/1951	Medicine Woman
Cybill Shepherd	2/18/1950	Moonlighting
Tom Selleck	1/29/1945	Magnum P.I., Blue Bloods

The only rule is don't be boring and dress cute
wherever you go. Life is too short to blend in.

Paris Hilton, born 2/17/1981

Aquarius Creativity Starters

- Experiment
- Create space
- Tackle a social issue
- Find a new application for the medium
- Move to a higher perspective
- Destroy and start again

Sports

- **Aquarius Sports Glimpses**
- **Sports Birthday Calendar**
- **Strong Mind's Eye**

- **Individual Genius**
- **Team Player**

Aquarius Sports Glimpses: Genius at Play

- Explosive Mary Lou Retton (1/24/1968) vaulting to Olympic gymnastics Gold

- Michael Jordan (2/17/1963) dominating both offensive and defensive ends of the basketball court

- Wayne Gretzky (1/26/1961) carrying the puck unchallenged behind the goal as opponents scramble to defend the passing lanes

- Near-perfect Olympic diving elegance from American Greg Louganis (1/29/1960)

- John McEnroe (2/16/1959) making another brilliant shot, throwing another on-court tantrum

- Popular golfer Greg Norman (2/10/1955) melting down at the Masters, giving up a six-stroke lead

- Swimmer Mark Spitz (2/10/1950) dominating the 1972 Olympics with a then-recordsetting seven Gold medals

- 46-year-old Jack Nicklaus (1/21/1940) charging through Augusta's back nine to win his sixth green jacket

- The slow, steady gait of football running back Jim Brown (2/17/1936), returning to the huddle after another spectacular carry

- Babe Ruth (2/6/1895) at home plate showing the direction of his next home run

Sports Birthday Calendar

Code	Sport / Role	Code	Sport / Role	Code	Sport / Role
A	Announcer	E	Executive	SC	Soccer
AR	Auto racing	F	Football	SK	Alpine skiing
BB	Baseball	FRS	Freestyle skiing	SRF	Surfing
BK	Basketball	G	Golf	SW	Swimming
BX	Boxing	GY	Gymnastics	SYN	Synch. Swimming
C	Coach	H	Hockey	T	Tennis
DN	Dance	J	Jockey	TF	Track and field
DV	Diving	SB	Snowboarding	WL	Weightlifting

January 20		Sport	January 21		Sport
1973	Eddie Kennison	F	1932	John Chaney	BK-C
			1940	Jack Nicklaus	G
			1963	Hakeem Olajuwon	BK
			1971	Doug Weight	H
			1984	Haloti Ngata	F
			1986	Payton Hillis	F

January 22		Sport	January 23		Sport
1904	George Balanchine	DN	1930	Mervyn Rose	T
1918	Elmer Lach	H	1936	Jerry Kramer	F

The Quotable Aquarius

1940	George Seifert	F-C	1967	Naim Suleymanoglu	WL
1955	Lester Hayes	F	1968	Eric Metcalf	F
1975	Felipe Giaffone	AR	1969	Brendan Shanahan	H
1982	Jason Peters	F	1971	Julie Foudy	SC
1987	Ray Rice	F	1989	Yani Tseng	G

January 24		Sport	January 25		Sport
1925	Maria Tallchief	DN	1924	Lou Groza	F
1968	Mary Lou Retton	GY	1941	Buddy Baker	AR
1987	Luis Suarez	SC	1942	Eusébio	SC
			1951	Steve Prefontaine	TF
			1980	Xavi	SC
			1984	Robinho	SC
			1985	Patrick Willis	F

January 26		Sport	January 27		Sport
1893	Frank Nighbor	H	1948	Mikhail Baryshnikov	DN
1907	Henry Cotton	G	1968	Matt Stover	F
1961	Wayne Gretzky	H	1968	Eric Wedge	BB-C
1977	Vince Carter	BK	1974	Ole Einar Bjoerndalen	B
			1976	Fred Taylor	F
			1980	Marat Safin	T
			1987	Hannah Teter	SB

January 28		Sport	January 29		Sport
1927	Jimmy Bryan	AR	1891	Richard Williams	T
1957	Nick Price	G	1923	Jack Burke	G
1974	Magglio Ordonez	BB	1945	Donna Caponi	G
1974	Kari Traa	FRS	1960	Greg Louganis	DV
1978	Gianluigi Buffon	SC	1964	Andre Reed	F
1984	Stephen Gostkowski	F	1965	Dominik Hasek	H
1985	Lisbeth Trickett	SW	1967	Sean Burke	H
			1973	Jason Schmidt	BB

January 30		Sport	January 31		Sport
1945	Curtis Strange	G	1908	Simone Mathieu	T
1957	Payne Stewart	G	1913	Don Hutson	F
			1916	Frank Parker	T
			1919	Jackie Robinson	BB
			1931	Ernie Banks	BB
			1947	Nolan Ryan	BB
			1957	Shirley Babashoff	SW
			1976	Buddy Rice	AR
			1984	Vernon Davis	F
			1985	Mario Williams	F
			1986	Walter Dix	TF

February 1		Sport	February 2		Sport
1915	Stanley Matthews	SC	1895	George Halas	F-C
1966	Michelle Akers	SC	1952	Dave Casper	F
1969	Gabriel Batistuta	SC	1975	Donald Driver	F

February 3		Sport	February 4		Sport
1940	Fran Tarkenton	F	1864	Willie Park Jr.	G
1941	Carol Mann	G	1912	Byron Nelson	G
1969	Retief Goosen	G	1959	Lawrence Taylor	F
1981	Kris Dielman	F	1963	Tracie Ruiz	SYN
			1973	Oscar De La Hoya	BX

February 5		Sport	February 6		Sport
1934	Hank Aaron	BB	1870	James Braid	G
1934	Don Cherry	H	1895	Babe Ruth	BB
1942	Roger Staubach	F	1985	Kris Humphries	BK
1947	Darrell Waltrip	AR			
1960	Jane Geddes	G			
1966	José Maria Olazabal	G			
1968	Roberto Alomar	BB			
1985	Cristiano Ronaldo	SC			

February 7		Sport	February 8		Sport
1966	Kristin Otto	SW	1954	Joe Maddon	BB-C
1974	Steve Nash	BK	1968	Joy Fawcett	SC
1988	Matt Stafford	F	1970	Alonzo Mourning	BK
			1990	Bethany Hamilton	SRF

February 9		Sport	February 10		Sport
1914	Bill Veeck	BB-E	1893	Bill Tilden	T
1958	Sandy Lyle	G	1950	Mark Spitz	SW
1961	John Kruk	BB	1955	Greg Norman	G
1976	Vladimir Guerrero	BB	1959	John Calipari	BK-C
			1974	Ty Law	F
			1976	Lance Berkman	BB
			1979	Ross Powers	SB
			1986	Seon-Hwa Lee	G
			1986	Viktor Troicki	T

February 11		Sport	February 12		Sport
1911	Helen Hicks	G	1881	Anna Pavlova	DN
1924	Budge Patty	T	1926	Joe Garagiola	BB-A
1971	Bruce Gardiner	H	1934	Bill Russell	BK
			1972	Owen Nolan	H

February 13		Sport	February 14		Sport
1918	Patty Berg	G	1913	Woody Hayes	F-C
1919	Eddie Robinson	F-C	1931	Bernie Geoffrion	H
1947	Mike Krzyzewski	BK-C	1935	Mickey Wright	G
1977	Randy Moss	F	1960	Jim Kelly	F
1982	Michael Turner	F	1972	Drew Bledsoe	F
			1976	Milan Hejduk	H
			1978	David Garrard	F
			1978	Richard Hamilton	BK

February 15		Sport	February 16		Sport
1866	Billy Hamilton	BB	1959	John McEnroe	T
1929	Graham Hill	AR	1972	Jerome Bettis	F
1972	Jaromir Jagr	H	1973	Cathy Freeman	TF
1983	Russell Martin	BB	1979	Sarah Lee	G

February 17		Sport	February 18		Sport
1934	Buddy Ryan	F-C	1895	George Gipp	F
1936	Jim Brown	F	1967	Roberto Baggio	SC
1959	Rowdy Gaines	SW	1971	Thomas Bjorn	G
1963	Michael Jordan	BK	1974	Yevgeny Kafelnikov	T
1970	Tommy Moe	SK			

February 19		Sport
1916	Eddie Arcaro	J

Strong Mind's Eye

The greatest sports achievements start in the mind. Aquarian intellect and perspective help the Aquarian athlete anticipate how the game will unfold. You're generally several steps ahead of your competition.

> *Never worry about missing a field goal. Just blame*
> *the holder and think about kicking the next one.*
> Lou Groza, born 1/25/1924

I knew what they all threw, and how hard, and where their release points were. I might not have known names and words the way sportswriters did, but I had a mental capacity at home plate that nobody seemed to appreciate. There's no such thing as a good hitter who is a dumb hitter . . . There are simply different kinds of intelligence, and I found out that if you don't express yours in the same way that the critics express theirs, then they

assume that you're dumb . . . Part of that natural ability was the natural ability to think in the batter's box.
Hank Aaron, born 2/5/1934

The ability to think clearly under pressure . . . If I had to pick the attribute that contributed most heavily to my golfing success it would be the ability to focus sharply and exclusively on the tasks at hand under the greatest competitive heat.
Jack Nicklaus, born 1/21/1940,
the first of Four Principles of Greatness

I've never missed a putt in my mind.
Jack Nicklaus, born 1/21/1940

Go to where the puck is going to be, not to where it is.
Wayne Gretzky, born 1/26/1961

*You have to expect things of yourselves
before you can do them.*
Michael Jordan, born 2/17/1963

Individual Genius

Aquarius contributes the "best-ever" legends of sport. No other zodiac sign comes close to Aquarius in sports genius. By doing it your way, you move the game to a higher level and raise the bar for the future.

Aquarius Specialty: Sports Superstars

Aquarius Superstar	Birthdate	Field of dominance
Michael Jordan	2/17/1963	Basketball
Wayne Gretzky	1/26/1961	Hockey
Greg Louganis	1/29/1960	Diving
John McEnroe	2/16/1959	Doubles tennis

Lawrence Taylor	2/4/1959	Defensive football
Mark Spitz	2/10/1950	Swimming
Nolan Ryan	1/31/1947	Baseball strikeouts
Jack Nicklaus	1/21/1940	Golf
Jim Brown	2/17/1936	Offensive football
Bill Russell	2/12/1934	Defensive basketball
Hank Aaron	2/5/1934	Baseball home runs, RBIs
Babe Ruth	2/6/1895	Baseball home runs, RBIs

*The greatest pleasure in life is doing
what people say you cannot do.*
Journalist Walter Bagehot, born 2/3/1826

*Alice laughed. "There's no use trying," she said. "One can't
believe impossible things." "I dare say you haven't had much
practice," said the Queen. "When I was your age, I always did it
for half an hour a day. Why, sometimes I've believed as many as
six impossible things before breakfast."*
Lewis Carroll, born 1/27/1832
Through the Looking-Glass

*Don't ask me how I do it. It always
comes out of me under pressure.*
Soccer star Stanley Matthews, born 2/1/1915,
when asked the secret of his skill

*Looking back, it's strange that nobody said anything about the
way I batted, which was cross-handed, with my left hand on top
even though I was right-handed. But the fact is, I don't think
anybody gave it a second thought. We were never told the right
way to bat, and we didn't lose any sleep over technique.*
Hank Aaron, born 2/5/1934

Great running is an art so intensely personal,
no two men do it quite alike. When a cat
makes a beautiful run, it's poetry and
jazz . . . Great runners are works of God.

Jim Brown, born 2/17/1936

I like people to make people stop and say "I've
never seen anyone run like that before!" It's
more than just a race, it's style. It's doing
something better than anyone else.

Steve Prefontaine, born 1/25/1951

I had a passion for getting out on the playground and being
my own person. I wanted to be different, to stand out. Playing
kickball and being the star because I was able to kick the ball
on top of a building, hitting home runs, stealing bases, pitching,
scoring 30 points, blocking a shot, dunking—all those things
drove me.

Michael Jordan, born 2/17/1963

There won't be another Jordan. There
won't be another Gretzky.

Jaromir Jagr, born 2/15/1972

Certain players are predisposed to creativity and decision making,
and I guess I'm one of them. I do believe that, to an extent, point
guards are born, not made. But you have to make yourself better.
You have to take those natural gifts and expand them.

Steve Nash, born 2/7/1974

You've got to have confidence and know you are
good. Then, just ride. I try to kill it in training,
then play it mellow in competition—though it is
definitely not mellow when you are in the halfpipe.
Hannah Teter, born 1/27/1987

Team Player

Despite individual greatness, Aquarians are team players. You apply your Aquarian concern for group welfare to the improvement of team dynamics. Basketball player-coach Bill Russell (2/12/1934) focused on optimizing team performance rather than individual performance. Russell's Boston Celtics won an unprecedented 11 league championships during Russell's 13-year career.

To be the best in the world. Not last week. Not next year. But
right now. You are the best. And it's even more satisfying as
a team, because that's more difficult. If I play well, that's one
thing. But to make others play better . . . You know what I mean?
Bill Russell, born 2/12/1934

The way a team plays as a whole determines
its success. You may have the greatest bunch of
individual stars in the world, but if they don't
play together, the club won't be worth a dime.
Babe Ruth, born 2/6/1895

I am proud of a few things. I've got the first, second, third, fourth,
fifth, sixth and seventh best assist years in league history. I'm
proud that I've either tied or led the league in assists every year
I've played. You do that and your teammates tend to like you.
Wayne Gretzky, born 1/26/1961

*Talent wins games, but teamwork and
intelligence win championships.*
Michael Jordan, born 2/17/1963

*You sit around with guys after a game, and you hear all these
ideas how to make things better. Then you wake up the next
day, and it's forgotten. I started thinking about [organizing a
meeting] after the Hall of Fame induction . . . I read comments
Coffey made [decrying] the state of the game. So I thought maybe
we should all talk about it. I called one player and one agent and
asked if a meeting like this could ever happen. They both told me
no. So I went ahead and tried to do it.*
Brendan Shanahan, born 1/23/1969,
credited with helping invigorate NHL rules

Aquarius Specialty: #1 in Football Legends

Aquarius contributes more legendary football players than any
other zodiac sign. These Aquarian football stars appear on vari-
ous lists of the greatest all-time football players and all-time record
holders.

Football Legend	Birthdate	Best-known Position
Randy Moss	2/13/1977	Minnesota/New England receiver
Fred Taylor	1/27/1976	Jacksonville running back
Ty Law	2/10/1974	New England cornerback
Jerome Bettis	2/16/1972	Pittsburgh running back, "The Bus"
Drew Bledsoe	2/14/1972	New England quarterback
Matt Stover	1/27/1968	Baltimore kicker
Eric Metcalf	1/23/1968	Cleveland running back
Andre Reed	1/29/1964	Buffalo receiver
Jim Kelly	2/14/1960	Buffalo quarterback
Lawrence Taylor	2/4/1959	Quick NY Giants linebacker

Dave Casper	2/2/1952	Oakland tight end
Roger Staubach	2/5/1942	Dallas quarterback
Fran Tarkenton	2/3/1940	Scrambling Minnesota quarterback
Jim Brown	2/17/1936	Cleveland running back
Don Hutson	1/31/1913	Green Bay wide receiver

The following contemporary Aquarius football stars are selected from top fantasy football rankings and recent Pro Bowl appearances. (Go to www.QuotableZodiac.com for astrological updates on all 21st-century sports stars.)

Football All-Star	Birthdate	Best-known Position
Matt Stafford	2/7/1988	Detroit quarterback
Ray Rice	1/22/1987	Baltimore running back
Payton Hillis	1/21/1986	Cleveland running back
Mario Williams	1/31/1985	Houston defensive end
Patrick Willis	1/25/1985	San Francisco linebacker
Vernon Davis	1/31/1984	San Francisco tight end
Stephen Gostkowski	1/28/1984	New England kicker
Haloti Ngata	1/21/1984	Baltimore defensive line
Michael Turner	2/13/1982	Atlanta running back
Jason Peters	1/22/1982	Buffalo tackle
Kris Dielman	2/3/1981	San Diego guard
David Garrard	2/14/1978	Jacksonville quarterback
Donald Driver	2/2/1975	Green Bay wide receiver
Ty Law	2/10/1974	Cornerback

Aquarius Baseball

Most all-time baseball player lists include the following Aquarians:

Baseball Legend	Birthdate	Known for:
Nolan Ryan	1/31/1947	Strikeouts
Hank Aaron	2/5/1934	Home run king
Ernie Banks	1/31/1931	Chicago shortstop, "Mr. Cub"
Jackie Robinson	1/31/1919	Breaking MLB's color barrier
Babe Ruth	2/6/1895	Home run king
Billy Hamilton	2/15/1866	Offensive records

I guess I just liked the game.

Babe Ruth, born 2/6/1895,
when asked the secret of his success

Baseball fans voted these contemporary players to Major League Baseball's All-Star roster on at least three occasions, with at least one appearance falling in the 21st century. Nontraditional Aquarius is the zodiac sign with the fewest contemporary baseball All-Stars.

Baseball All-Star	Birthdate	Known for:
Russell Martin	2/15/1983	Dodger and Yankee catcher
Lance Berkman	2/10/1976	Houston and St. Louis hitter
Vladimir Guerrero	2/9/1976	Ability to hit any pitch
Magglio Ordonez	1/28/1974	Detroit hitter
Jason Schmidt	1/29/1973	Los Angeles pitcher
Roberto Alomar	2/5/1968	Cleveland second baseman

Aquarius Basketball

This list includes Aquarians typically named to all-time basketball player lists and those earning NBA Most Valuable Player honors.

Basketball MVP	Birthdate	Best-known Position
Steve Nash (2x)	2/7/1974	Phoenix point guard
Michael Jordan (5x)	2/17/1963	Chicago all-star
Hakeem Olajuwon	1/21/1963	Houston center
Bill Russell (5x)	2/12/1934	Boston center and leader

In addition to the MVPs listed above, these Aquarians have earned at least three NBA All-Star appearances, with one or more falling in the 21st century.

Basketball All-Star	Birthdate	Best-known Position
Richard Hamilton	2/14/1978	Detroit shooting guard
Vince Carter	1/26/1977	Orlando guard/forward
Alonzo Mourning	2/8/1970	Miami center

Aquarius Specialty: #1 Hockey MVP Awards

Led by nine-time winner Wayne Gretzky, innovative Aquarius has earned more pro hockey MVP awards than any other zodiac sign. Hardworking Virgo has more hockey MVP winners but fewer total awards.

Hockey MVP	Birthdate	Best-known Position
Jaromir Jagr	2/15/1972	Pittsburgh right wing
Dominik Hasek (2x)	1/29/1965	Buffalo goalie
Wayne Gretzky (9x)	1/26/1961	Edmonton center
Bernie Geoffrion	2/14/1931	Montreal right wing
Elmer Lach	1/22/1918	Montreal center
Frank Nighbor	1/26/1893	Ottawa center

*Maybe it wasn't talent the Lord gave
me. Maybe it was the passion.*
Wayne Gretzky, born 1/26/1961

Aquarius places second among zodiac signs in number of players who have earned at least three recent appearances in professional hockey's annual All-Star game.

Hockey All-Star	Birthdate	Best-known Position
Marian Gaborik	2/14/1982	New York forward
Dany Heatley	1/21/1981	San Jose forward
Milan Hejduk	2/14/1976	Colorado forward
Owen Nolan	2/12/1972	San Jose wing
Mats Sundin	2/13/1971	Toronto captain
Doug Weight	1/21/1971	Role model forward
Brendan Shanahan	1/23/1969	New York forward
Sean Burke	1/29/1967	Goalie

Aquarius Specialty: #1 in Soccer Stars

Another sport where Aquarian athletes rank first! Inventive, team-oriented Aquarius contributes more famous soccer players than any other astrological sign. Aquarius contributed the pioneering members of the U.S. women's soccer program.

Soccer Player	Birthdate	Nationality and Position
Luis Suárez	1/24/1987	Uruguayan striker
Cristiano Ronaldo	2/5/1985	Portuguese striker
Robinho	1/25/1984	Brazilian forward
Xavi	1/25/1980	Spanish midfielder
Gianluigi Buffon	1/28/1978	Italian goalkeeper
Julie Foudy	1/23/1971	American midfielder
Gabriel Batistuta	2/1/1969	Argentinian striker

Joy Fawcett	2/8/1968	American defender
Roberto Baggio	2/18/1967	Italian striker
Michelle Akers	2/1/1966	American midfielder
Eusébio	1/25/1942	Portuguese forward
Stanley Matthews	2/1/1915	English outside right, Wizard of Dribble

Aquarius Coaches

Duke coach Mike Krzyzewski (2/13/1947) has earned the most wins in collegiate basketball history. Legendary Grambling football coach Eddie Robinson (2/13/1919) was beloved by many of his players for his guidance in both football and life. But several Aquarian coaches are as well-known for temperamental outbursts as for team accomplishments. Woody Hayes (2/14/1913) was forced to retire after punching an opposing player. Philadelphia Eagles coach Buddy Ryan (2/17/1934) was accused of taking out a bounty on opposing players.

I'll kill you. You remember that, I'll kick your ass! You've got a good team and you don't need that edge! That's why I told my kid to knock your f----- kid in the mouth!
John Chaney, born 1/21/1932,
to John Calipari (2/10/1959) after an altercation between the two

Aquarius Coach	Birthdate	Best-known Coaching Position
Eric Wedge	1/27/1968	Cleveland / Seattle baseball
John Calipari	2/10/1959	College basketball
Joe Maddon	2/8/1954	Tampa Bay Rays baseball
Mike Krzyzewski	2/13/1947	Duke basketball
George Seifert	1/22/1940	Two Super Bowls
Buddy Ryan	2/17/1934	Philadelphia Eagles football
John Chaney	1/21/1932	Temple basketball
Eddie Robinson	2/13/1919	Grambling football
Woody Hayes	2/14/1913	Ohio State football
George Halas	2/2/1895	Chicago Bears football

Aquarius Olympians

Independent Aquarian athletes specialize in swimming and in nontraditional solitary sports. Aquarian innovation shines through in emerging Olympic events such as synchronized swimming, moguls and halfpipe.

Aquarius Athlete	Birthdate	Country	Known for:
Hannah Teter	1/27/1987	USA	Snowboard halfpipe Gold
Walter Dix	1/31/1986	USA	2 track sprint medals
Lisbeth Trickett	1/28/1985	Australia	6 swimming medals
Ross Powers	2/10/1979	USA	Snowboard halfpipe Gold
Kari Traa	1/28/1974	Norway	Moguls medals (3 consecutive)
Ole Einar Bjoerndalen	1/27/1974	Norway	11 biathlon medals
Cathy Freeman	2/16/1973	Australia	400-meter track Gold
Tommy Moe	2/17/1970	USA	Downhill Gold
Mary Lou Retton	1/24/1968	USA	Gymnastics Gold
Naim Suleymanoglu	1/23/1967	Turkey	Weightlifting Gold (3 consecutive)
Kristin Otto	2/7/1966	Germany	6 swimming Golds
Tracie Ruiz	2/4/1963	USA	3 synchronized swimming medals
Greg Louganis	1/29/1960	USA	4 diving Golds
Rowdy Gaines	2/17/1959	USA	3 swimming Golds
Shirley Babashoff	1/31/1957	USA	8 swimming medals
Mark Spitz	2/10/1950	USA	9 swimming Golds

I want to be remembered as a strong and graceful diver. But as a person, I want to be remembered as someone who made a difference.
Greg Louganis, born 1/29/1960

Aquarius Specialty: #1 in Golf Champions

With special capacity for handling the unexpected, Aquarius earns the most major golf championships for both men and women.

The following list of Aquarian golf champions includes only those Aquarians who have won at least two majors. Women's majors include the British Open, U.S. Open, LPGA Championship, Kraft and several earlier events that have since been de-emphasized. Only four women's major championships have been held each year. The men's major championships are the British Open, U.S. Open, PGA Championship and The Masters.

Golf Champion	Birthdate	Country	# Majors
Jack Nicklaus	1/21/1940	USA	18
Patty Berg	2/13/1918	USA	15
Mickey Wright	2/14/1935	USA	13
Yani Tseng	1/23/1989	Taiwan	5
Byron Nelson	2/4/1912	USA	5
James Braid	2/6/1870	Scotland	5
Donna Caponi	1/29/1945	USA	4
Payne Stewart	1/30/1957	USA	3
Nick Price	1/28/1957	South Africa	3
Henry Cotton	1/26/1907	England	3
Retief Goosen	2/3/1969	South Africa	2
José Maria Olazabal	2/5/1966	Spain	2
Jane Geddes	2/5/1960	USA	2
Sandy Lyle	2/9/1958	Scotland	2
Greg Norman	2/10/1955	Australia	2
Curtis Strange	1/30/1945	USA	2
Carol Mann	2/3/1941	USA	2
Jack Burke	1/29/1923	USA	2
Helen Hicks	2/11/1911	USA	2
Willie Park Jr.	2/4/1864	Scotland	2

A bad bounce, a gust of wind, a spiked-up green,
a twinge in your hip, a spasm in your back—any
of them can bring you undone in an instant.

Jack Nicklaus, born 1/21/1940

Golf Contender	Birthdate	Country
Seon-Hwa Lee	2/10/1986	South Korea
Stacy Lewis	2/16/1985	USA
Sarah Lee	2/16/1979	South Korea

Aquarius Tennis

Here are the Aquarians who have won at least two major championships. Major tennis events are Wimbledon, the Australian Open, the French Open and the U.S. Open.

Aquarius Champion	Birthdate	Country	# Majors
Bill Tilden	2/10/1893	USA	10
John McEnroe	2/16/1959	USA	7
Frank Parker	1/31/1916	USA	4
Marat Safin	1/27/1980	Russia	2
Yevgeny Kafelnikov	2/18/1974	Russia	2
Mervyn Rose	1/23/1930	Australia	2
Budge Patty	2/11/1924	USA	2
Simone Mathieu	1/31/1908	France	2
Richard Williams	1/29/1891	USA	2

Never change a winning game;
always change a losing one.

Bill Tilden, born 2/10/1893

Tennis Contender	Birthdate	Country
Viktor Troicki	2/10/1986	Serbia

Aquarius Boxing

Boxer	Birthdate	Known for:
Oscar De La Hoya	2/4/1973	5-time world champ

Aquarius Dancing

Aquarius Dancer	Birthdate	Known for:
Mikhail Baryshnikov	1/27/1948	Ballet / modern
Maria Tallchief	1/24/1925	First U.S. prima donna
George Balanchine	1/22/1904	NYC Ballet choreography
Anna Pavlova	2/12/1881	The Dying Swan

> *I do not try to dance better than anyone else.*
> *I only try to dance better than myself.*
> Mikhail Baryshnikov, born 1/27/1948

Aquarius Auto Racing

Here are the Aquarius winners of the Daytona 500, the Indy 500 (since 1946), and the NASCAR series now called the Sprint Cup.

Aquarius Driver	Birthdate	Event(s) Won
Buddy Rice	1/31/1976	Indy 500
Darrell Waltrip	2/5/1947	Daytona 500, Sprint Cup (3x)
Buddy Baker	1/25/1941	Daytona 500
Graham Hill	2/15/1929	Indy 500
Jimmy Bryan	1/28/1926	Indy 500

> *You know the risks, you accept them. If a man can't look at danger and still go on, man has stopped living. If the worst ever happens—then it means simply that I've been asked to pay the bill for the happiness of my life—without a moment's regret.*
> Graham Hill, born 2/15/1929

Spirituality

- **Respect**
- **Action**
- **Tolerance**
- **New Age**

- **Nature**
- **Spirit Realms**
- **Purification**

Aquarius Religious Figures

Religious Figure	Birthdate	Known as:
Allison DuBois	1/24/1972	Crime psychic (TV's "Medium")
Eckhart Tolle	2/16/1948	Popular spiritual writer
Carlos Belo	2/3/1948	Bishop awarded Nobel Peace prize
Oral Roberts	1/24/1918	Founder of evangelical church
Emanuel Swedenborg	2/8/1688	Swedish scientist and mystic
Cotton Mather	2/12/1663	New England Puritan minister
Thomas More	2/7/1478	Reformation martyr
Thomas Aquinas	1/28/1225	Catholic theologian

Respect

Aquarians generally accept the contributions of a supreme being. You respect the higher powers and strive to work alongside the divine plan.

We can't have full knowledge all at once. We must start by believing; then afterwards we may be led on to master the evidence for ourselves.

Thomas Aquinas, born 1/28/1225

I had rather believe all the fables in the legend, and the Talmud, and the Alcoran, than that this universal frame is without a mind.

Francis Bacon, born 1/22/1561

There is a grandeur in this view of life, with its several powers, having been originally breathed by the Creator into a few forms or into one, and that . . . from so simple a beginning endless forms most beautiful and most wonderful have been and are being evolved.

Charles Darwin, born 2/12/1809
On the Origin of Species

God alone can finish.

John Ruskin, born 2/8/1819

How would man exist if God did not need him, and how would you exist? You need God in order to be, and God needs you—for that is the meaning of your life.

Martin Buber, born 2/18/1878
I and Thou

*The highest point a man can attain is not Knowledge,
or Virtue, or Goodness, or Victory, but something even
greater, more heroic and more despairing: Sacred Awe!*

Nikos Kazantzakis, born 2/18/1883
Zorba the Greek

*I've always believed that we are, each of us, put here for
a reason, that there is a . . . divine plan for all of us.*

Ronald Reagan, born 2/6/1911

*We have what we seek, it is there all the time, and if we give it
time, it will make itself known to us.*

Thomas Merton, born 1/31/1915

*What I know is there is a calling on each of our lives, a sacred
contract that each of us made with the creator when we came
into being. It is each of our jobs to find out what that is and get
on about the business of doing it.*

Oprah Winfrey, born 1/29/1954

*Spirituality takes some of the significance off the things that are
traps for people, like the material world. It lightens the load so
you can face things with joy rather than fear. People fear a job
or not having an ideal body and if they can move away from that
and think, "Oh, cool, I got a body to play with," that's much
healthier. Religion and spirituality are becoming more popular.
Why? Because there's nothing else to look at after you've looked
at this universe and said, "What else?" If you only look at things
on a scientific level, you're only getting 50 percent of the story. If
you're spiritual, it doesn't matter what you ascribe to. People can
connect with each other on that commonality alone.*

John Travolta, born 2/18/1954

Aquarius Specialty: 20th-Century Influence

Aquarius ties Libra with four of the top 25 most influential religious figures of the 20th century as named by a leading magazine. Libra and Aquarius are the social activists of the zodiac.

20th-Century Religious Figure	Birthdate	Known as:
Thomas Merton	1/31/1915	Writer on spirituality and social justice
Carl F.H. Henry	1/22/1913	Christianity Today magazine founder
Dietrich Bonhoeffer	2/4/1906	Hitler assassination attempt
Martin Buber	2/18/1878	Scholar, Israeli nationalist

Action

Aquarians insist that spirituality include actions to enhance societal well-being. German pastor and theologian Dietrich Bonhoeffer (2/4/1906) perceived Hitler as pure evil. Bonhoeffer plotted to kill Hitler, but was apprehended and executed.

Better to illuminate than merely to shine, to deliver to others contemplated truths than merely to contemplate.
                              Thomas Aquinas, born 1/28/1225

The things, good Lord, that we pray for,
Give us the grace to labor for.
                              Thomas More, born 2/7/1478

But men must know that in this theater of man's life it is reserved only for God and angels to be lookers on.
                              Francis Bacon, born 1/22/1561

April 26. Welcome, O life! I go to encounter for the millionth time the reality of experience and to forge in the smithy of my soul the uncreated conscience of my race.
April 27. Old father, old artificer, stand me now and ever in good stead.

James Joyce, born 2/2/1882
A Portrait of the Artist as a Young Man

We are given one life and the decision is ours whether to wait for circumstances to make up our mind or whether to act, and in acting, to live.

Omar Bradley, born 2/12/1893

If you know what life is worth, you will look for yours on earth.

Bob Marley, born 2/6/1945

Striving for the defense of the rights of all peoples is not only the privilege of those guiding the destiny of the people or those enjoying lofty positions in society, but it is the duty of the duty of everyone whatever rank or status.

Carlos Belo, born 2/3/1948

"How" is always more important that "what." See if you can give much more attention to the doing than to the result that you want to achieve through it.

Eckhart Tolle, born 2/16/1948

The truth is that while I was waiting on God, God was waiting on me. He was waiting on me to make a decision to either pursue the life that was meant for me or be stifled by the one I was living.

Oprah Winfrey, born 1/29/1954

It doesn't matter what you have if you don't have a feeling of doing something good for other people. The more you give, the more you're filled up. I get to have that feeling in my life every single day. I meet people who tell me, "I was in the hospital and I was so sick. I watched you every day, and you helped me feel better." Or, "I lost my husband and I watched you and you made me feel better." Those stories that I get, everybody that tells me that they got something good from me, it's all that I need.

Ellen DeGeneres, born 1/28/1958

Give without hesitation.
Snowboarder Hannah Teter, born 1/27/1987,
asked what words she lived by

Tolerance

The Water-Bearer rains equally upon all. Today's Water-Bearers continue the historical Aquarian practice of religious tolerance.

Beware of the person of one book.
Thomas Aquinas, born 1/28/1225

*This is one of the ancientest laws among
them: that no man shall be blamed for
the maintenance of his own religion.*
Thomas More, born 2/7/1478
Utopia

One religion is as true as another.
Robert Burton, born 2/8/1577

*I fully believe that it is the will of the
Almighty that there should be a diversity
of religious opinion among us.*
Thomas Paine, born 2/9/1737
Common Sense

Why paradise necessitates exclusion.
Toni Morrison, born 2/18/1931,
on the question addressed in her book Paradise

Because of religious indoctrination, almost everyone feared and loathed the serpent. What damage had such hatred done to it; a magical expression of Creation? . . Hunted and killed, or killed instantly, on sight, forced to hide at all times, what did the serpent think of humanity? Why had women, long ago, befriended the serpent, loved it? Why had Cleopatra had asps as pets?
Alice Walker, born 2/9/1944
Now Is the Time to Open Your Heart

New Age

The Earth now moves into the Age of Aquarius after about 2000 years in the Age of Pisces, aptly symbolized by the Christian fishes. The Age of Aquarius breaks away from traditional religion. Aquarians are early adopters of the new approaches to spirituality.

I do not believe in the creed professed by the Jewish church, by the Roman church, by the Greek church, by the Turkish church, by the Protestant church, nor by any church that I know of. My own mind is my own church.
Thomas Paine, born 2/9/1737
The Age of Reason

There is something pagan in me that I cannot shake off. In short, I deny nothing, but doubt everything.
Lord Byron, born 1/22/1788

I read the book of Job last night—I don't think God comes well out of it.
Virginia Woolf, born 1/25/1882

There's a natural mystic blowing through the air.
Bob Marley, born 2/6/1945

*I definitely would be (from) Mars. I would say I'm
Venus sometimes . . . I'd say I'm more from the moon.*
Cybill Shepherd, born 2/18/1950
saying she's not sure where she's from

*I have the distinct feeling that I chose my family . . . In
the next [lifetime] I may be even more causative.*
John Travolta, born 2/18/1954

*I got kicked out of Bible school. I was always joking
and laughing. They finally just said, "Get out of here." I
went home crying, "They kicked me out for laughing."*
Chris Rock, born 2/7/1965

*I've had everything from deep laughter to deep sadness,
where I was crying through moves. It's good to get
that stuff out. You feel like you're having a therapy
session, a workout and a meditation at the same time.*
Jennifer Aniston, born 2/11/1969

*I think I have. I was a much older 13 than most. I'm like, dang, I
wish I would have just been a regular 12-year-old. I wish I didn't
always take everything on my shoulders so heavy. And still, even
musically, I feel I connect with the '0s and '0s. Maybe in some
way I was alive then, and came back for this time now.*
Alicia Keys, born 1/25/1981,
asked if she thought she'd lived before

*Anything that has to do with rejuvenation of mind,
body and spirit, I'm all for it: a spa or a great massage.*
Alicia Keys, born 1/25/1981

Aquarius Specialty: New Age Habits

With greater incidence than other signs, Aquarians practice techniques commonly labeled "new age."

- W. Somerset Maugham (1/25/1874) explored rejuvenation therapy
- President Ronald Reagan (2/6/1911) consulted an astrologer on a regular basis
- Painter Jackson Pollock (1/28/1912) pursued theosophy and Native American healing
- Mia Farrow (2/9/1945) has studied Zen, ESP, yoga and transcendental meditation
- Actress Marisa Berenson (2/15/1947) believes in reincarnation
- Cybill Shepherd (2/18/1950) uses the healing powers of crystals
- Jane Seymour (2/15/1951) was married by Marianne Williamson, Hollywood's New Age guru
- Hockey star Jaromir Jagr (2/15/1972) has claimed that he channels the universe's energy sources into his body

Nature

Aquarians gravitate to open space. With greater frequency and acceptance than other zodiac signs, environmentally-aware Aquarians link religion to the wonders of nature.

By confronting us with irreducible mysteries that
stretch our daily vision to include infinity, nature opens
an inviting and guiding path toward a spiritual life.
Thomas More, born 2/7/1478

*Nature, to be commanded, must be obeyed. In
everything man has accomplished, we have only
manipulated nature into doing what it is.*
Francis Bacon, born 1/22/1561

I am always most religious upon a sunshiny day.
Lord Byron, born 1/22/1788

*Man has been endowed with reason, with the power to create, so
that he can add to what he's been given. But up to now he hasn't
been a creator, only a destroyer. Forests keep disappearing, rivers
dry up, wild life's become extinct, the climate's ruined and the
land grows poorer and uglier every day.*
Anton Chekhov, born 1/29/1860
Uncle Vanya

*Men have an extraordinarily erroneous opinion of
their position in nature; and the error is ineradicable.*
W. Somerset Maugham, born 1/25/1874

*Oh, how one wishes sometimes to escape
from the meaningless dullness of human
eloquence, from all those sublime phrases, to
take refuge in nature, so inarticulate.*
Boris Pasternak, born 2/10/1890
Doctor Zhivago

*In wilderness I sense the miracle of life, and behind
it our scientific accomplishments fade to trivia.*
Charles Lindbergh, born 2/4/1902

When you a child of the mountains yourself, you really belong to them. You need them. They become the faithful guardians of your life. If you cannot dwell on their lofty heights all your life, if you are in trouble, you want at least to look at them.

Maria von Trapp, born 1/26/1905

By reading the scriptures I am so renewed that all nature seems renewed around me and with me. The sky seems to be a pure, a cooler blue, the trees a deeper green. The whole world is charged with the glory of God and I feel fire and music under my feet.

Thomas Merton, born 1/31/1915

I think it pisses God off if you walk by the color purple in a field somewhere and don't notice it . . . People think pleasing God is all God care about. But any fool living in the world can see it always trying to please us back.

Alice Walker, born 2/9/1944
The Color Purple

She had an instinctive understanding, perhaps from birth, that people and plants were relatives. As a child she had spent hours talking to, caressing, sitting in, kissing, and otherwise trying to communicate with trees. As a very young child she'd been convinced that trees had mouths and that she could find a mouth on a tree if only she grew tall enough and looked for it very hard.

Alice Walker, born 2/9/1944
Now Is the Time to Open Your Heart

The most important thing, without getting corny, is it puts you in touch with the weather, the soil, nature. You start thinking in a way that I don't think is a bad thing in modern society.

Tom Selleck, born 1/29/1945,
about working his avocado ranch

If everything else went away, as long as I've saved
enough money that I can live with trees and animals
around, that's the most important thing to me.
Ellen DeGeneres, born 1/28/1958

Spirit Realms

Aquarians bypass the apparent physical barriers. Many of you acknowledge direct communication with ghosts and guardian spirits. Scientist Thomas Edison (2/11/1847) tried to develop a phone for communication between the living and the dead. Aquarian Allison DuBois (1/24/1972) is a real-life crime psychic whose cases formed the basis of the television series *Medium*.

Every human being has, like Socrates, an
attendant spirit; and wise are they who obey
its signals. If it does not always tell us what to
do, it always cautions us what not to do.
Lydia Child, born 2/11/1802

Whatever may be the origin of the cause of
the rappings, the ladies in whose presence
they occur do not make them.
Horace Greeley, born 2/3/1811,
about seances with the Fox sisters

By believing passionately in something that still
does not exist, we create it. The nonexistent is
whatever we have not sufficiently desired.
Nikos Kazantzakis, born 2/18/1883

Some time, Rock, when the team's up against it, when things are
wrong and the breaks are beating the boys—tell them to go in
there with all they've got and win just one for the Gipper.

George Gipp, born 2/8/1895,
Dying request, to coach Knute Rockne

I felt my father's presence. He was a doctor
whose passion was the history of medicine.
As his eldest daughter, he raised me to learn
everything about his work. So I did Dr. Quinn.

Jane Seymour, born 2/15/1951

The only thing that scares me more than space aliens
is the idea that there aren't any space aliens. We
can't be the best that creation has to offer. I pray
we're not all there is. If so, we're in big trouble.

Ellen DeGeneres, born 1/28/1958

I still write him letters and that separation,
that ability to communicate with the
dead, is very much a part of Jeffrey.

Greg Louganis, born 1/29/1960,
about his stage role as Jeffrey

When I feel confused about a decision and over a night's period
I feel like I've come up with a solution, I feel like I've gotten
spiritual input from my father. It gives me the confidence to make
a decision instinctively, whatever the decision may be.

Michael Jordan, born 2/17/1963

*I always knew I was strong and that I had to
keep going. And I came to learn that as much as
was taken away from me, I've also been given so
much. I have some serious guardian angels.*

Mariska Hargitay, born 1/23/1964

*I saw a ghost while [rehearsing] a play at New York's Belasco
Theater. I looked up and in the upper balcony was a woman in
a blue satin dress with blonde crimped hair. It didn't scare me. I
turned, did my line and when I looked back, she was gone. I told
the house manager, "I saw a ghost." He said, "Blue dress, blonde
hair? Yeah, you did."*

Laura Linney, born 2/5/1964

*Somebody's watching out for me. I believe in
that. I believe in God. I don't think we are that
great that this just happened on our own.*

Jennifer Aniston, born 2/11/1969

Purification

Aquarius on the zodiac wheel brings purification before the cleansing depths of Pisces and the fresh birth of Aries. As the Sun moves through Aquarius, Catholics bless the home candles at Candlemas and Celts observe the Imbolc feast of purification. With your capacity for abrupt transition, Aquarius emerges onto the next level with renewed perspective.

*We shall find peace. We shall hear the angels,
we shall see the sky sparkling with diamonds.*

Anton Chekhov, born 1/29/1860
Uncle Vanya

Better pass boldly into that other world,
in the full glory of some passion, than
fade and wither dismally with age.

James Joyce, born 2/2/1882

Just head for that big star, it will take us home.

Clark Gable, born 2/1/1901
The Misfits

If a man can bridge the gap between life
and death, if he can live on after he's dead,
then maybe he was a great man.

James Dean, born 2/8/1931

Far, we've been traveling far without
a home, but not without a star.

Neil Diamond, born 1/24/1941

I can't accept that you live and die and that's
it. I was born with a Karma and what I make
of this life will put me closer to God in the next.
My ultimate goal is to become a saint.

Marisa Berenson, born 2/15/1947

I'm going to a special place when I die, but I want
to make sure my life is special while I'm here.

Payne Stewart, born 1/30/1957

Firewalking is part of my process. Rebirthing
is part of my process. I follow the medicine
path and I attend sweat lodges, an ancient
Native American ceremony of purification.

LeVar Burton, born 2/16/1957

Aquarius Tarot Card: The Star

Metaphysical tradition links Aquarius to the Tarot card The Star. The standard Tarot card shows stars above a figure pouring water. The Star card represents the spiritual intelligence and insight to dispense the radiant energy of the Universe.

Maturity

- **Moving to a New Level**
- **Transcending Body**
- **Still Contributing**
- **Eccentric to the End**

Moving to a New Level

Maturing Aquarians approach the advancing years as new plateaus for living. With the Aquarian capacity for sharp transition, you simply shift gears to another level. At age 74, Gene Hackman (1/30/1931) retired from acting to write novels. Tom Selleck (1/29/1945) and Vanessa Redgrave (1/30/1937) have developed different onscreen personalities in their later years.

> *A comfortable old age is the reward of a well-spent youth. Instead of its bringing sad and melancholy prospects of decay, it would give us hopes of eternal youth in a better world.*
>
> Lydia Child, born 2/11/1802

The older I get, the greater power I seem to
have in the world; I am like a snowball—
the further I am rolled, the more I gain.
Susan B. Anthony, born 2/15/1820

One does not get better but different and
older and that is always a pleasure.
Gertrude Stein, born 2/3/1874

People think that their world will get smaller as they
get older. My experience is just the opposite. Your
senses become more acute. You start to blossom.
Yoko Ono, born 2/18/1933

I'm ready to try some new things.
That's what life is all about.
Tom Brokaw, born 2/6/1940,
upon retirement

Our take on life is different at every stage of
our lives. We just have to commit ourselves to
seeing who we are as clearly as we can.
Alice Walker, born 2/9/1944

My advice for women entering menopause is to trust your
feelings. Explore. Invest in yourself, whether it be through school
or therapy or church. Believe in yourself, find out who you are. As
a woman out there today, you have to be a warrior.
Cybill Shepherd, born 2/18/1950

I am going to rock it out. I feel like it is just
the beginning of a whole new level for me.
Oprah Winfrey, born 1/29/1954,
on turning 50

Transcending Body

Mind over matter. Your intellect deepens and your already-broad perspective expands even more. The mental power of Aquarius increases with age.

It is really mortifying to be so corporeal, that we cannot stir a step without dragging this tenement of clay about with us. You will tell me, perhaps, that the imagination travels a great way; that we think, and this is, in reality, the same thing. No, no, my dear; there is a wide difference.

Madame de Sévigné, born 2/5/1626

The tree of deepest root is found
Least willing still to quit the ground:
'Twas therefore said by ancient sages,
That love of life increased with years
So much, that in our latter stages,
When pain grows sharp and sickness rages,
The greatest love of life appears.

Hester Lynch Piozzi, born 1/27/1741
Three Warnings

Let me advise thee not to talk of thyself as being old. There is something in Mind Cure, after all, and, if thee continually talks of thyself as being old, thee may perhaps bring on some of the infirmities of age. At least I would not risk it if I were thee.

Hannah Whitall Smith, born 2/7/1832

In spite of illness, in spite even of the archenemy sorrow, one can remain alive long past the usual date of disintegration if one is unafraid of change, insatiable in intellectual curiosity, interested in big things, and happy in small ways.

Edith Wharton, born 1/24/1862

Imagination grows by exercise, and contrary
to common belief, is more powerful in
the mature than in the young.

W. Somerset Maugham, born 1/25/1874

When the Lord calls me home, I will leave with the greatest love
for this country of ours and eternal optimism for its future. I now
begin the journey that will lead me into the sunset of my life. I
know that for America there will always be a bright dawn ahead.
Thank you, my friends. May God always bless you.

Ronald Reagan, born 2/6/1911
Letter to America after his Alzheimer's diagnosis

It's smart not to think you're "old." Mature, maybe, but
never old. Keep doing, keep fighting, keep swinging.
Get out there—keep resisting your limitations.

Jack Nicklaus, born 1/21/1940

Still Contributing

Aquarius thrives on contributing to humanity. After providing seminal literature for the women's liberation movement, 72-year-old Betty Friedan (2/4/1921) published *The Fountain of Age*. The book debunks the notion of age as decline, instead providing evidence of ordinary people in their sixties and seventies reaching new heights of intimacy and purpose.

When I embarked upon the ten-year ordeal of writing, I
found an age mystique even more pervasive, pernicious,
perverted and obsolete than the feminine mystique.

Betty Friedan, born 2/4/1921

*To do the work that you are capable of
doing is the mark of maturity.*
Betty Friedan, born 2/4/1921

Neither lemonade nor anything else can prevent the inroads of old age. At present, I am stoical under its advances, and hope I shall remain so. I have but one prayer at heart; and that is, to have my faculties so far preserved that I can be useful, in some way or other, to the last.
Lydia Child, born 2/11/1802

*Look at all of your knowledge as a gift, as a
means of helping other people. A strong and wise
person uses his gifts to support other people*
John Ruskin, born 2/8/1819

*What am I supposed to do with my 75 years
of experience? Am I supposed to bury it?*
Civil rights pioneer Juanita Craft, born 2/9/1902

*Hell, I'm not going to stagnate. I want
to get going and do things.*
Ernest Borgnine, born 1/24/1917

*At 50, you know a lot more than you did when you
were 25, so you can use all that stuff you didn't know
to propel yourself forward. I feel like [turning 50]
is everything you were meant to be in your life.*
Oprah Winfrey, born 1/29/1954

Eccentric to the End

Watch for the Aquarian's inherent silly streak. Aquarians continue to surprise with unexpected behavior.

"You are old, Father William," the young man said,
"And your hair has become very white;
And yet you incessantly stand on your head—
Do you think, at your age, it is right?"

Lewis Carroll, born 1/27/1832
Alice in Wonderland

One keeps forgetting old age up to
the very brink of the grave.

Colette, born 1/28/1873
My Mother's House

Words to Live By

Do not worry; eat three square meals a day; say your prayers; be courteous to your creditors; keep your digestion good; exercise; go slow and easy. Maybe there are other things your special case requires to make you happy; but, my friend, these I reckon will give you a good lift.

Abraham Lincoln, born 2/12/1809

*Have a heart that never hardens, a temper
that never tires, a touch that never hurts.*

Charles Dickens, born 2/7/1812

*Speak in French when you can't think of
English for a thing—turn out your toes when
you walk—and remember who you are.*

Lewis Carroll, born 1/27/1832

*Be grateful for luck. Pay the thunder no mind—
listen to the birds. And don't have nobody.*

Eubie Blake, born 2/7/1883

Live in the moment and treasure every breath. I know for sure that to be present with yourself is the most important gift you can have. Appreciate now, so that the next hour and the next year don't slip away unnoticed. Every moment matters.
Oprah Winfrey, born 1/29/1954

There is no comparison between that which is lost by not succeeding and that lost by not trying.
Francis Bacon, born 1/22/1561

Nothing valuable can be lost by taking time.
Abraham Lincoln, born 2/12/1809

The highest reward for a person's toil is not what they get for it, but what they become by it.
John Ruskin, born 2/8/1819

There is no substitute for hard work.
Thomas Edison, born 2/11/1847

Success depends in a very large measure upon individual initiative and exertion, and cannot be achieved except by a dint of hard work.
Anna Pavlova, born 2/12/1881

The only thing that separates successful people from the ones who aren't is the willingness to work very, very hard.
Helen Gurley Brown, born 2/18/1922

Man is born to live, not to prepare for life.
Boris Pasternak, born 2/10/1890

Hold fast to dreams, for if dreams die, life is
a broken winged bird that cannot fly.
Langston Hughes, born 2/1/1902

Begin somewhere; you cannot build a
reputation on what you intend to do.
Liz Smith, born 2/2/1923

Dream as if you'll live forever. Live as if you'll die today.
James Dean, born 2/8/1931

Doing the best at this moment puts you in
the best place for the next moment.
Oprah Winfrey, born 1/29/1954

Whatever you are, be a good one.
Abraham Lincoln, born 2/12/1809

Sunshine is delicious, rain is refreshing, wind braces us
up, snow is exhilarating; there is really no such thing
as bad weather, only different kinds of good weather.
John Ruskin, born 2/8/1819

Make one's center of life inside one's self, not selfishly
or excludingly, but with a kind of unassailable serenity.
Edith Wharton, born 1/24/1862

You do what you can for as long as you can,
and when you finally can't, you do the next best
thing. You back up but you don't give up.
Chuck Yeager, born 2/13/1923

You should live a life with as few negatives
as possible—without acquiescing.
Bill Russell, born 2/12/1934

Some have meat and cannot eat,
Some cannot eat that want it:
But we have meat and we can eat,
Sae let the Lord be thankit.

Robert Burns, born 1/25/1759

Gratitude is the memory of the heart; therefore
forget not to say often, I have all I ever enjoyed.

Lydia Child, born 2/11/1802

Reflect on your present blessings, of which
every man has many; not on your past
misfortunes, of which all men have some.

Charles Dickens, born 2/7/1812

Keep a grateful journal. Every night, list five things
that you are grateful for. What it will begin to do is
change your perspective of your day and your life.

Oprah Winfrey, born 1/29/1954

My good luck charm is my gratitude. Every night I go
to sleep and I'm grateful for my life, and I wake up and
I feel the same thing. I just accept everything as it is—
whatever happens is what I'm supposed to deal with.

Ellen DeGeneres, born 1/28/1958

Be happy. It is a way of being wise.

Colette, born 1/28/1873

Let unconquerable gladness dwell.

Franklin Roosevelt, born 1/30/1882

*How simple and frugal a thing is happiness: a glass of
wine, a roast chestnut, a wretched little brazier, the
sound of the sea . . . All that is required to feel that
here and now is happiness is a simple, frugal heart.*
Nikos Kazantzakis, born 2/18/1883

*What is all this running around after happiness? Why don't we
just do something constructive, something creative, and then if
that makes us happy, fine. If it doesn't, at least we still have tilled
the garden, baked the bread, taken care of somebody or written
the book.*
Toni Morrison, born 2/18/1931

*Do something that makes you happy,
and it shows in your physical self.*
Molly Ringwald, born 2/18/1968

Go easy, and if you can't go easy, go as easy as you can.
Gertrude Stein, born 2/3/1874

Selected Bibliography

Aaron, Hank with Lonnie Wheeler, *I Had a Hammer*, HarperCollins Publishers, New York, 1991.

Compiled and arranged by Abby Adams, *An Uncommon Scold*, Simon and Schuster, New York, 1989.

Amende, Coral, *Hollywood Confidential*, Plume (imprint of Dutton Sargent, div Penguin Books), New York, 1997.

Edited by John Bartlett and Justin Kaplan, *Bartlett's Familiar Quotations*, Little, Brown and Company, Boston, 1992.

Burt, Kathleen, *Archetypes of the Zodiac*, Llewellyn Worldwide Ltd., St. Paul, Minnesota, 1990.

Edited by James Charlton, *The Military Quotation Book*, Thomas Dunne Books (imprint of St. Martin's Press), New York, 2002.

Deger, Steve, *The Boy's Book of Positive Quotations*, Fairview Press, Minneapolis, 2009.

Deger, Steve and Leslie Ann Gibson, *The Girl's Book of Positive Quotations*, Fairview Press, Minneapolis, 2008.

De Vito, Carlo, *The Ultimate Dictionary of Sports Quotations*, Checkmark Books, New York, 2001.

Goldschneider, Gary, *The Secret Language of Relationships*, Penguin Studio, New York, 1997.

Goodman, Linda, *Linda Goodman's Sun Signs*, Bantam Books, New York, 1968.

Greene, Liz, *The Astrology of Fate*, Samuel Weiser Inc., York Beach, Maine, 1984.

Gretzky, Wayne with Rick Reilly, *Gretzky: An Autobiography*, An Edward Burlingame Book (HarperCollins Publishers), New York, 1990.

Grisham, John, *The Street Lawyer*, Bantam Dell, New York, 1998.

Hellstern, Melissa, *Getting Along Famously*, Dutton (member of Penguin Group), New York, 2008.

Jackson, Gordon, S., *Never Scratch a Tiger with a Short Stick*, NavPress, Colorado Springs, 2003.

Jagendorf, M. A., *Stories and Lore of the Zodiac*, The Vanguard Press Inc., New York, 1977.

Edited by Elizabeth Knowles, *The Oxford Dictionary of Phrase, Saying, and Quotation*, Oxford University Press, New York, 1997.

Compiled by Glenn Liebman, *2,000 Sports Quips and Quotes*, Gramercy Books, New York, 1993.

Compiled by Rosalie Maggio, *The Beacon Book of Quotations by Women*, Beacon Press, Boston, 1992.

Compiled by J. Michael Mahoney, *Topsy Turvy*, AuthorHouse, Bloomington, Indiana, 2009.

McEnroe, John with James Kaplan, *You Cannot Be Serious*, G.P. Putnam's Sons, New York, 2002.

Edited by Peter McWilliams, *The LIFE 101 Quote Book*, Prelude Press, Los Angeles, 1996.

Edited by John Miller and Aaron Kenedi, *lovers*, a Bulfinch Press Book, Little, Brown and Company, New York, 1999.

Nicklaus, Jack with Dr. John Tickell, *Golf & Life*, St. Martin's Press, New York, 2003.

Oken, Alan, *Alan Oken's Complete Astrology*, Bantam Books, New York, 1988.

The Oxford Dictionary of Quotations, Oxford University Press, New York, 1979.

Palin, Sarah, *Going Rogue*, HarperCollins Publishers, New York, 2009.

Compiled by Charles Panati, *Words to Live By*, Penguin Books, New York, 1999.

Parker, Derek and Julia, *Sun & Moon Signs*, DK Publishing Inc., New York, 1996.

Compiled and edited by Elaine Partnow, *The Quotable Woman From Eve to 1799*, Facts on File Publications, New York, 1985.

Pickering, David, *Cassell's Sports Quotations*, Cassell & Co, London, 2000.

Rand, Ayn, *Atlas Shrugged*, Signet, New York, 2007.

Edited by Connie Robertson, *The Wordsworth Dictionary of Quotations*, Wordsworth Editions Ltd., Ware, Hertfordshire, Great Britain, 1998.

Edited by Kate Rowinski, *The Quotable Mom*, Main Street (division of Sterling Publishing Co. Inc.), New York, 2004.

Compiled by George Seldes, *The Great Quotations*, Lyle Stuart, New York, 1960.

Edited by John M. Shanahan, *The Most Brilliant Thoughts of All Time*, Cliff Street Books (an imprint of HarperCollins Publishers), New York, 1999.

Edited and introduced by Jessie Shiers, *The Quotable Bitch*, The Lyons Press, Guilford, Connecticut, 2008.

Smart Mouths, Portable Press, Ashland, Oregon, 2009.

Edited by Marlo Thomas, *The Right Words at the Right Time*, Atria Books, New York, 2002.

Edited by Jonathan Waterman, *The Quotable Climber*, The Lyons Press, New York, 1998.

Weekes, Karen, *Women Know Everything!*, Quirk Books, Philadelphia, 2007.

Compiled and edited by Jon Winokur, *True Confessions*, Dutton, New York, 1992.

The Quotable Aquarius

Index of Aquarians

G

Gable, Clark 18, 93, 100, 107, 114, 118, 128, 153, 193
Gabor, Zsa Zsa 19, 72, 78
Gaines, Rowdy 164, 175
Garagiola, Joe 78, 163
Garcia, Anastasio Somoza 18, 133
Gardiner, Bruce 52, 163
Garrard, David 163, 170
Geddes, Jane 162, 176
Geneen, Harold 16, 123, 133, 134
Geoffrion, Bernie 163, 172
Getty, Balthazar 16, 157
Getz, Stan 18, 151, 153
Giaffone, Felipe 161
Gipp, George 155, 164, 191
Glass, Philip 18, 149
Gompers, Sam 17, 124
Goosen, Retief 162, 176
Gostkowski, Stephen 161, 170
Graham, Heather 17, 95
Grant, Julia 16, 106
Greeley, Andrew 19
Greeley, Horace 19, 122, 149, 190
Greene, Lorne 21
Greer, Germaine 17, 36, 48, 53, 57, 62, 79, 81, 96
Gretzky, Wayne 17, 51, 52, 61, 68, 85, 113, 127, 159, 161, 165, 168, 172, 173, 207
Grey, Zane 17, 148
Griffith, D.W. 16, 118, 135, 142, 154
Grisham, John 20, 36, 62, 67, 68, 74, 78, 102, 148, 207
Groening, Matt 22, 147
Groza, Lou 161, 164
Guercino 20, 147
Guerrero, Vladimir 163, 171
Guest, Christopher 20, 107
Gwyn, Nell 18, 117

H

Hackman, Gene 18, 93, 119, 153, 195
Halas, George 162, 174
Hall, Arsenio 21, 158
Halsey, Margaret 22, 81, 140
Hamilton, Bethany 163
Hamilton, Billy 164, 171
Hamilton, Richard 163, 172
Hanover, Donna 22, 117
Hargitay, Mariska 16, 62, 114, 119, 120, 156, 157, 192
Harrison, William Henry 20, 119, 123
Hart, Johnny 23, 147
Hasek, Dominik 161, 172
Havens, Richie 15
Hayes, Lester 161
Hayes, Woody 22, 163, 174
Heifetz, Jascha 18, 84
Hejduk, Milan 163, 173
Helms, Ed 16, 157
Henderson, Florence 22, 41
Henry, Carl F.H. 16, 182
Hershey, Barbara 20, 92, 93, 114
Hicks, Helen 163, 176
Highmore, Freddie 22, 156
Hilbert, David 15, 134
Hill, Benny 15
Hill, Graham 164, 178
Hillis, Payton 160, 170
Hilton, Paris 23, 52, 108, 110, 111, 112, 117, 143, 157, 158
Hines, Gregory 22, 85
Hoffa, Jimmy 22, 124
Holbrook, Hal 23, 156
Hopkins, Mark 19
Hughes, Langston 18, 84, 148, 203
Humphries, Kris 20, 104, 117, 162
Hurt, John 16
Hutson, Don 162, 170

M

MacArthur, Douglas 16, 43, 62, 82, 106, 133
Maddon, Joe 163, 174
Maher, Bill 15
Mailer, Norman 18, 39, 59, 78, 98, 118, 138
Malone, Dorothy 17, 154
Manet, Edouard 15, 141, 147
Mankiewicz, Joseph 21, 142
Mann, Carol 162, 176
Mann, Delbert 17, 142
Mansart, François 15, 147
Margolin, Stuart 18, 156
Marley, Bob 20, 35, 39, 183, 186
Martin, Dick 17, 110
Martin, Russell 164, 171
Mather, Cotton 21, 179
Mathieu, Simone 162, 177
Matthews, Stanley 162, 166, 174
Maugham, W. Somerset 16, 30, 43, 45, 76, 77, 80, 89, 98, 148, 149, 187, 188, 198
McCormack, Mary 20
McCormick, Cyrus 22, 134
McDonald, Michael 21, 150
McEnroe, John 22, 28, 57, 60, 63, 73, 75, 85, 107, 108, 110, 116, 159, 164, 165, 177, 208
McKinley, William 17, 117, 123
McLachlan, Sarah 17, 60, 151, 152
Mendelssohn, Felix 19, 150
Meredith, George 21
Merton, Thomas 18, 97, 181, 182, 189
Metcalf, Eric 161, 169
Michener, James 19, 148
Moder, Danny 18, 107
Moe, Tommy 164, 175
Moody, D.L. 19, 122
Moreau, Jeanne 16
More, Hannah 18, 65, 82, 125
More, Thomas 20, 43, 44, 89, 149, 155, 179, 182, 184, 187
Morita, Akio 17, 133
Morris, Heather 18, 63, 128
Morrison, Toni 23, 28, 31, 73, 84, 94, 135, 140, 148, 155, 185, 205
Moss, Randy 72, 79, 163, 169
Mourning, Alonzo 163, 172
Mozart, Wolfgang Amadeus 16, 48, 76, 84, 135, 141, 142, 150, 155

N

Najimy, Kathy 20, 108
Nash, Steve 163, 167, 172
Nelson, Byron 162, 176
Newman, Paul 17, 33, 35, 61, 62, 110, 112, 119, 146, 153
Ngata, Haloti 160, 170
Nicklaus, Jack 15, 39, 53, 74, 90, 111, 126, 160, 165, 166, 176, 177, 198, 208
Nielsen, Leslie 21
Nighbor, Frank 161, 172
Nolan, Owen 163, 173
Nolte, Nick 20
Norman, Greg 21, 51, 74, 104, 115, 159, 163, 176

O

O'Connell, Jerry 23, 107, 157
Olajuwon, Hakeem 160, 172
Olazabal, José Maria 162, 176
Olbermann, Keith 17, 69
Onassis, Athina 17, 157
Ono, Yoko 23, 50, 117, 138, 151, 196
Ordonez, Magglio 161, 171
Orianthi 16, 86
Otto, Kristin 163, 175
Overstreet, Chord 23, 108

About the Author

Mary Valby's fascination with astrology began as she wrote her Princeton thesis on medieval zodiac signs. Mary has since filtered thousands of books, birthdates, and celebrity comments according to Sun sign. Her astrological pursuits include personalized birth-chart readings, ten years maintaining an astrological website, and membership in the American Federation of Astrologers. Raised in upstate New York, Mary now enjoys the Pacific Northwest.

Mary Valby's Astrological Beliefs

- **Real vs. Imaginary.** Astrology works. After cataloguing thousands of celebrities and reading hundreds of charts, Mary fully accepts that astrological placements and movements impact each individual. The celestial sphere proves one of Nature's many guiding cycles.

- **Sun Sign vs. Full Birth-Chart.** The most comprehensive celestial snapshot of your potential comes from a full astrological birth-chart based on time of birth and referencing all solar system planets. The zodiac location of the Sun at your birth indicates far less but remains meaningful. Your Sun sign describes your core energy, the driving life-force that underlies the rest of your personality.

- **Self-Knowledge vs. Prediction.** The better use of astrology is as a tool for self-knowledge. You are not the same as other people; how can you build upon your personal talents while minimizing your weaknesses? Astrology's prediction of favorable and unfavorable periods is most accurate when calculated from a full astrological birth-chart.

- **Free Will vs. Determinism.** Astrology suggests rather than dictates. As if playing a hand of cards, you remain free to choose your responses and actions.

Sun Sign	Usual Dates
Aries	March 21 through April 19
Taurus	April 20 through May 20
Gemini	May 21 through June 20
Cancer	June 21 through July 21
Leo	July 22 through August 22
Virgo	August 23 through September 21
Libra	September 22 through October 22
Scorpio	October 23 through November 22
Sagittarius	November 23 through December 21
Capricorn	December 22 through January 19
Aquarius	January 20 through February 18
Pisces	February 19 through March 20

The dates shown above are the most typical dates for the Sun's yearly passage through each zodiac sign. But the Sun moves into each sign at a specific moment each year, with the dates varying by a day or two from year to year. If you are unsure about the Sun sign for yourself or a person of interest, send date, time and place of birth to help@quotablezodiac.com for a free zodiac identification.

Quick Order Form

Website orders: www.quotablezodiac.com.
Major credit cards accepted.
Email orders: orders@quotablezodiac.com
Postal orders: Quotable Zodiac Publishing, LLC
Mary Valby, P.O. Box 2011, Gig Harbor, WA 98335, USA.
Please send check or money order.
Telephone orders: 253-858-6372, have credit card ready.
The Quotable Zodiac Series

Please send the following books:
____The Quotable Libra ($12.95)
____The Quotable Scorpio ($12.95)
____The Quotable Sagittarius ($12.95)
____The Quotable Capricorn ($12.95)
____The Quotable Aquarius ($12.95)
____The Quotable Pisces ($12.95)
____The Quotable Aries ($12.95)
____The Quotable Taurus ($12.95)
____The Quotable Gemini ($12.95)—available March 2013
____The Quotable Cancer ($12.95)—available March 2013
____The Quotable Leo ($12.95)—available March 2013
____The Quotable Virgo ($12.95)—available March 2013
____Shipping (U.S.): $4.00 for first book and
         $2.00 for each additional book
____Shipping (International): $9.00 for first book,
         $5.00 for each additional book
____Total

Name: _____

Address: _____

City:_____State:_____Zip:_____

Telephone:_____

Email address:_____

Send questions or comments to info@thequotablezodiac.com

Sun Sign	Usual Dates
Aries	March 21 through April 19
Taurus	April 20 through May 20
Gemini	May 21 through June 20
Cancer	June 21 through July 21
Leo	July 22 through August 22
Virgo	August 23 through September 21
Libra	September 22 through October 22
Scorpio	October 23 through November 22
Sagittarius	November 23 through December 21
Capricorn	December 22 through January 19
Aquarius	January 20 through February 18
Pisces	February 19 through March 20

The dates shown above are the most typical dates for the Sun's yearly passage through each zodiac sign. But the Sun moves into each sign at a specific moment each year, with the dates varying by a day or two from year to year. If you are unsure about the Sun sign for yourself or a person of interest, send date, time and place of birth to help@quotablezodiac.com for a free zodiac identification.

Quick Order Form

Website orders: www.quotablezodiac.com.
Major credit cards accepted.
Email orders: orders@quotablezodiac.com
Postal orders: Quotable Zodiac Publishing, LLC
Mary Valby, P.O. Box 2011, Gig Harbor, WA 98335, USA.
Please send check or money order.
Telephone orders: 253-858-6372, have credit card ready.
The Quotable Zodiac Series

Please send the following books:

____The Quotable Libra ($12.95)
____The Quotable Scorpio ($12.95)
____The Quotable Sagittarius ($12.95)
____The Quotable Capricorn ($12.95)
____The Quotable Aquarius ($12.95)
____The Quotable Pisces ($12.95)
____The Quotable Aries ($12.95)
____The Quotable Taurus ($12.95)
____The Quotable Gemini ($12.95)—available March 2013
____The Quotable Cancer ($12.95)—available March 2013
____The Quotable Leo ($12.95)—available March 2013
____The Quotable Virgo ($12.95)—available March 2013
____Shipping (U.S.): $4.00 for first book and
   $2.00 for each additional book
____Shipping (International): $9.00 for first book,
   $5.00 for each additional book
____Total

Name: _____

Address: _____

City:_____State:_____Zip: _____

Telephone:_____

Email address: _____

Send questions or comments to info@thequotablezodiac.com